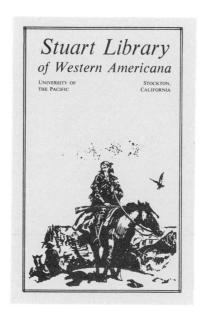

CUSTER'S LAST

CUSTER'S LAST

or,

The Battle of the Little Big Horn

In Picturesque Perspective
Being a pictorial representation
of the late and unfortunate

INCIDENT IN MONTANA

as portrayed by Custer's friends and
foes, admirers and iconoclasts
of his day
and after

DON RUSSELL

AMON CARTER MUSEUM OF WESTERN ART BOARD OF TRUSTEES

The Amon Carter Museum of Western Art was established
under the will of the late Amon G. Carter for the study
and documentation of westering North America.
The program of the Museum is expressed in publications,
exhibitions, and permanent collections related to the
many aspects of American culture, both historic and
contemporary, which find their identification as Western.

Mitchell A. Wilder, Director, Amon Carter Museum of Western Art

ACKNOWLEDGMENTS

This book would never have happened except for the suggestion of Mitchell A. Wilder, director of the Amon Carter Museum of Western Art, Fort Worth. He contemplated an exhibition from a hundred or so Custer's Last Stand pictures with an accompanying explanatory book. His patience and encouragement while the book and concomitant list of pictures all too slowly grew and grew and grew has my gratitude. That gratitude extends also to the Museum's curator of history, Miss Barbara Tyler, who never once, as months stretched into years, gave any intimation that anything was more important to her than Custer and pictures about him, although obviously she was concerned with other subjects, other exhibitions, and other interests. She is responsible for numerous additions to the list and for running down many of the originals. To other members of the Museum's board and staff who took me in as a sort of *ex officio* colleague, my sincere thanks.

Readers may be curious as to how such an off-beat idea ever got started in the first place. I started with Mrs. Cassilly Adams II, Lina Adams, of Silver Spring, Maryland, who wrote to me after I had written an editorial deploring the burning up of the "Custer's Last Fight" painted by her father-in-law. She generously shared her accumulation of source material about him. The result was an article in *The Westerners Brand Book*, which received some subsequent publicity. The story might have stopped there, but I began to discover that I had become the acknowledged expert on Custer Fight pictures. How far off I was from being "expert", I discovered some hundreds of Custer pictures later. Knowledge of these hundreds came from a devoted band of Custer collectors and enthusiasts who shared their duplicates, took photographs, compiled long lists, loaned rare books, and otherwise put me deeply in debt to their generosity.

Topping my list of those without whom there would be many gaps in the record are, in alphabetical order: Joseph Balmer of Zurich, Switzerland; Brian W. Dippie, Austin, Texas; John S. duMont, Greenfield, Massachusetts; John C. Ewers, Smithsonian Institution; Dr. Lawrence Frost, Monroe, iv

Michigan; Michael Harrison, Fair Oaks, California; John C. Hixon, Palm Desert, California; James S. Hutchins, Vienna, Virginia; J. E. Leithead, Philadelphia, for most of what appears about dime novels; Frank L. Mercatante, Grand Rapids, Michigan; Melvin J. Nichols, Summit, New Jersey; Hugh W. Shick, North Hollywood, California; the late Elmo Scott Watson; Chester J. Yatcek, Midway City, California.

Among artists and members of their families, I have had generous help from: Roland F. Becker, son of F. Otto Becker; Thomas Hart Benton, Lorence F. Bjorklund, Wood M. Cowan, Hermann Eber, son of Elk Eber; Brummett Echohawk, Nick Eggenhofer, the late R. Farrington Elwell, Joe Grandee, the late Gayle Porter Hoskins, Stanley Legowik, Ken Lizorty, Walter S. Oschman, William Edgar Paxson, son of Edgar Samuel Paxson; T. B. Pitman, Jr., son of Theodore Baldwin Pitman, J. K. Ralston, Ernest L. Reedstrom.

Our thanks also for the generous help of: Betty Baker, editor, WWA Roundup; Charles Bragin, Brooklyn; Marshall Davidson, Metropolitan Museum of Art, Roy E. Dunne. Chicago; Doris Flowers of Julian Messner, Inc.; Stella A. Foote, Billings, Montana; George E. Hyde, Omaha; J. Leonard Jennewein, Mitchell, South Dakota; Michael Kennedy; Betty B. Lockwood, San Rafael, California; Thomas Millstead, Racine, Wisconsin; Joseph G. Rosa, Ruislip, Middlesex, England; Bert Sheldon, Washington, D.C.; J. C. Simms, General Mills, Inc., Minneapolis; the late General Edward J. Stackpole, Harrisburg, Pennsylvania; J. W. Todd, Jr., Shorey Book Store, Seattle; Mary W. Williams, Museum of the American Indian, New York.

CONTENTS

CUSTER'S LAST

PREFACE

How many paintings do you suppose there are of the Custer battle on the Little Big Horn? This question was posed about four years ago by our Director, Mitchell A. Wilder, who seems to have an insatiable curiosity for such things. His question was serious enough, but the atmosphere of researching it was more like a game. We could count ten such paintings by name on our fingers quickly. A 30-minute search through the Museum library produced twenty-five more. How curious, we thought, that so many illustrations should proliferate from a catastrophe that no man survived to describe (excepting the Indians, of course). But that in itself was a clue to the popularity of the subject—no one knew what had happened, there-fore, to each his own opinion and to each the right to impose that opinion on others. Naturally, our next question was whether or not we could bring together enough of the paintings for an exhibition, and, if so, who knew enough about the subject to prepare a manuscript.

We tucked the idea away and waited for a likely candidate to appear. Within six months we were again talking seriously about Custer paintings, this time with Don Russell, a well-known colleague in the history field, who immediately informed us that there were at least 200 representations of Custer's last fight. Our problem, he informed us, was not in naming them, but in finding them, and he was right.

We engaged Don as special consultant and all set to work. Three and a half years later, we are able to exhibit 200 illustrations of Custer's Last Stand, but they are not necessarily the original 200 on our checklist. In the course of those research years, over 600 additional illustrations have come to light, many of them having been done since we started to work on the project. Hardly a month went by that a dozen or more were not added to the list. We soon learned that Custer's popularity among graphic artists was not limited to the painters of over-sized canvases. He was just as popular to the New York advertising firm who needed a good gimmick to catch the public eye; to the cartoonist who wished to link his fictitious characters to a folk hero; to the promotion experts who were not satisfied with plain bubble gum wrappers, milk bottle tops or whiskey bottle labels; to the writers and illustrators of juvenile and adult fiction; and to the recurring generations of Custer buffs who do, indeed, continue to turn up new facts, which mean new articles and books, which, of course, command new illustrations. Sad, but true, as this book goes to press an untold number are on the drawing board and easel!

The purpose of this publication and exhibition is not to rehash the pros and cons of the Custer controversy, but to point out that, because of the controversial circumstances surrounding the Custer fight and a surfeit of unknown elements which shaped that fateful day, a continuing portrayal of the event has become a stock item in American history. It was a relatively unimportant battle, in a quiet time in history, made famous by and for the needs of posterity. The Battle of the Little Big Horn is world-renowned and Custer is recognized by some as a hero and by others as the perpetrator of one of the world's most famous military blunders. We may marvel at the growth of this pictorial fantasy, but we do not dispute the fact that the event has become legend, and recognize that our efforts only add to the perpetuation of that legend. We would not for a moment suppose that *Custer's Last* will be!

Barbara Tyler
Curator of History

THE LEGEND

No single event in United States history, or perhaps in world history, has been the subject of more bad art and erroneous story than Custer's Last Stand at the Battle of the Little Big Horn on June 25, 1876.

A search by no means exhaustive turns up 848 pictures relating to that fight—a lot of picture making for a happening of so little importance. Despite the Chinese cliché that a picture is worth a thousand words, many of these pictures are accompanied by many more than a thousand words of misinformation.

Not all of the art is bad. The subject has attracted able artists. Not all of the writing is bad. The mystery and the tragedy have interested conscientious and painstaking historians. But the desire to depict what might have happened, or to explain how it happened, accounts for only a small percentage of the total output. The attraction and the interest have been so universal that many fools rush in, unaware of the many traps that strew the way. With mercenary motive fiction is turned into fable and lies into legends. Yet after all this interment of fact, folklore and folk art cling tenaciously to the essentially heroic interpretation.

In the long run, both dramatization and debunkery fail of permanent impression. The residue left to the general public may be scant in detail, but sure in identification. To almost every American, to almost everyone who knows anything about America, a reference to Custer's Last Stand is meaningful. A cartoonist may put over his idea by citing Custer as quickly and as surely as by use of many another convention of his craft. An advertiser finds effective message power in the Last Stand whether used seriously or facetiously.

The late President Kennedy in the last year of his life twice made points by references to the Custer fight. At Bonn, Germany, on June 23, 1963, he said in paying tribute to Chancellor Adenauer: "When he was born in 1876, Bismarck was chancellor of Germany and Ulysses S. Grant was President of the United States. And two years after his birth, to indicate how young the United States is, General Custer and 500 of his cavalry were to be wiped out by Sitting Bull and the Sioux Indians."

He was wrong about the date, and wrong about the casualty figure, but undoubtedly right in assuming that no event that occurred in the United States in the period would be more readily recognized in Germany.

Again at Salt Lake City on September 26, in speaking of the test-ban treaty, President Kennedy remarked: "It may be as I said, that we may fail, but anyone who bothers to look at the true destructive power of the atom today, and what we and the Soviet Union could do to each other in an hour and in a day, and to Western Europe—I passed over yesterday the Little Big Horn where Custer was slain, a massacre which has lived in history, 400 or 500 men—we are talking about 300 million men and women in 24 hours."

The casualty figure is still wrong, and there has been much objection to calling it a "massacre," but President Kennedy proved that it has "lived in history" and he was right in stressing its relative unimportance.

The Little Big Horn was not one of the world's fifteen, or fifteen hundred, decisive battles. It decided nothing. According to some military standards it does not deserve even to be called a battle. It is more commonly—and more authentically—called a "fight." It had no lasting effect on a war that was not a war, legally or officially. The Indians won, but gained nothing by their victory, nor could they. There is little evidence that the troops were spurred to greater efforts by the disaster; they were not largely reinforced; they won no considerable retaliatory victories. The campaign of which the Little Big Horn fight was a part dragged on in its dreary and unspectacular course—and within a few months the Sioux had ceased to retard the march of progress, if it *was* progress.

It would have been little different had there been no Custer's Last Stand.

It came at a relatively quiet time in world history. Life in the later years of the 19th century seems idyllic, at least to those who only read about it. It was a time when any unusual occurrence—a scandal involving the Rev. Henry Ward Beecher, the kidnaping of Charlie Ross, the Johnstown flood, the wreck on the Monon—was long remembered, discussed, mulled over. But President Kennedy could have made no point in Bonn or in the Mormon Tabernacle by mention of Beecher, Charlie Ross, Johnstown or the Monon.

What gives the Custer story its vitality after nine decades?

School texts and general histories that for a half-century contributed a considerable share of Last Stand art are now almost silent on the subject.

In many of them the name of Custer does not appear. By no means is this to be regarded as added proof of the unimportance of the Little Big Horn. Professors and schoolmen shy away from anything that smacks of legendary heroics. They are equally wary of Buffalo Bill, Wild Bill, Sitting Bull, Geronimo, Jesse James, or Wyatt Earp—names almost any man on the street will recognize as linked to the epic of the West. Custer has gained little of his current notoriety from the schoolroom.

A few decades ago the man on the street could, by merely passing through a pair of swinging doors and buying a nickel beer, get a lasting lesson in the legendry of Custer's Last Fight. But the gory barroom lithography that for decades was conversation piece in the poor man's club is inappropriate to the décor of the dimly lighted cocktail lounge. The painting by Cassilly Adams that Adolphus Busch presented to the Seventh Cavalry has been burned to a cinder and F. Otto Becker's adaptation of it for purposes of pictorial reproduction is found only in the back rooms of antique dealers—and infrequently there.

How is it then that the average American knows about, and thinks he knows all about, Custer's Last Stand?

More has been written, painted, drawn, carved, and moulded to depict the Little Big Horn fight than has been done to explain Saratoga, Gettysburg, San Juan Hill, Chateau Thierry, D-Day, Iwo Jima, or the Inchon Landing, and very likely more than for all of them together. Bodies of the victims were only half-buried when Captain Frederick Whittaker, a prolific writer of dime novels, came out in 1876 with a volume two inches thick including gold-embossed binding called *A Complete Life of Gen. George A. Custer.*

His use of the adjective "complete" was not widely accepted. Few years have since gone by that have not seen publication of books and magazine articles all hopefully offering new interpretations of Custer and the Little Big Horn. The flow of ink over the name of Custer never stops. New books appeared while these pages were being written. Few days pass without mention of Custer's name in newspapers.

Recent pulp-magazine titles reveal the constant search for the new and sensational. Top prize for effort might go to "Did a Woman Die with Custer?" The question-mark title has an advantage: the question need not be answered. Other examples are: "Which Indian Killed Custer?" and "Could Custer Have Won?" However, "Did Cholera Defeat Custer?" was no product of the pulps that intersperse Western shockers with poses of the topless bathing suit and other scantily clad females. It was found in *Surgery, Gynecology, and Obstetrics,* official journal of the American

College of Surgeons, for May, 1947, along with "Treatment of Tricho-
monas Vaginalis Vaginitis" and the like.

"The Day Custer Massacred the Indians" is about the Battle of the
Washita, but other deprecatory titles are "The Bloody Hands of General
Custer," "Suicide on the Little Big Horn," "Custer's Troop of Doom," and
"Custer's Folly." A surprising number are much less imaginative, even
to such a hardy perennial as "The True Story of Custer's Last Stand."
Unhappily, "Last Word on Custer's Last Stand" was not.

Little tads who find no mention of Custer in their social-studies texts
are not kept in ignorance of the campaign against the Sioux. A bubble-
gum card of a few years back featured a portrait of Custer and was
accompanied by a red transparency which, when placed over the back of
the card, revealed an answer to the question: "What happened to Custer's
army at the Battle of Big Horn?" with a depiction quite as accurate as
the query. This bubble-gum series included Buffalo Bill, Wild Bill, Sitting
Bull, Geronimo, Jesse James, Wyatt Erp, and other characters neglected
by social scientists.

A certificate rescued from a sack of flour brings you a jigsaw puzzle of
"Famous American Landmarks," said landmarks being the Boston Tea
Party, the Liberty Bell, the Alamo, Sutter's Mill, Gettysburg, and—Custer's
Last Stand. A less sophisticated, if more international, choice was offered
in a series of cutouts printed on breakfast-food boxes. The full repertoire
was Goldilocks, Three Little Pigs, Jack and the Beanstalk, Little Red
Ridinghood, King Arthur's Knights, Robin Hood, Treasure Island, and—
Custer's Last Stand. Educational Posters (1959) offers in its series suitable
for schoolroom decoration "Winning the West" in which the subjects are
Lewis and Clark, Battle of the Alamo, Frontier Marshal, and—Custer's
Last Stand. Milk bottles also go into schoolrooms, and an entrepreneur
supplied milk-bottle caps depicting historic American dates. Of 24 subjects,
nine related to wars, mentioning four battles: Fort Sumter as the
beginning of the Civil War, Pearl Harbor as the beginning of World War
II, the Alamo, and—"Massacre of General Custer in Battle of the Little
Big Horn."

That children become confused among folklore, legendry, and history
is not astonishing—especially when they come across such items as a
"Historical Play Money" series featuring, among others, General Custer
and Sitting Bull. Concerning Sitting Bull it is explained: "On June 25,
1876, his warriors attacked the U.S. Cavalry men under General Custer,
killing all. This was the Battle of Bull Run;" [sic.,] a professional historian
would insert here, meaning, you can hardly believe it, but so it is.

Every schoolboy knows that he cannot depend upon the history that is to be found on a giveaway gimmick, but many a book approved for social studies supplementary reading might lead him quite as far astray. In a book called, with some lack of originality, *Custer's Last Stand*, a correspondent from the battlefields of World War II, the late Quentin Reynolds, set up Sitting Bull as Supreme Commander (the capitals are his) and provided him with a communications center complete with walkie-talkies on horseback: "Sitting Bull was in his lodge getting reports. He had been getting them all morning (page 167) . . . Walking Hawk touched the right side of his forehead with his left hand, in the Sioux salute to a chief, leaped to his horse and headed for Crazy Horse" (page 168). Soon (page 174) he was back to report: "Crazy Horse says he has lost five hundred men." By this time "Sitting Bull was getting half-hour reports," and by page 182, "scouts came every fifteen minutes now with reports," timed, no doubt, by their waterproof wrist watches.

Sitting Bull's part in the fight has been controversial ever since the Indian agent James McLaughlin asserted that Sitting Bull was off in the hills making medicine. This juvenile thriller leaves him little time for medicine-making between those 15-minute reports. As for the Crazy Horse holocaust, an early Sioux account, that of Red Horse, comes up with a figure of 136 Indians killed. Stanley Vestal's check of Indian sources cut this back to 36.* This seems far too low, but 500 is far too high.

Unhappily this book is typical rather than exceptional in its scorn for facts in the pap that is fed to youngsters in the guise of history and biography. Books about Custer—or about Sitting Bull, or Crazy Horse, or the horse, Comanche, are standard items; a half dozen or so are in print. Few are more reliable as history than were their predecessors that had been frankly labeled juvenile fiction.

Dime novels, romantic fiction, motion pictures, and television have contributed to the Custer legend. There is a vast bibliography on the Battle of the Little Big Horn—how else could there be all these pictures—yet Custer biographies have been shockingly few and largely superficial.

It has become common to downgrade Custer as rash, reckless, irresponsible, arrogant, incompetent, insubordinate, and unscrupulous. In many cases writers have based such judgments on their interpretation of the Little Big Horn without reference to Custer's previous career, particularly his Civil War record, which has received little attention, and frequently

---

Tenth Annual Report of the Bureau of Ethnology, 1888-'89, Government Printing Office, Washington, 1893, p. 566; Stanley Vestal, *New Sources of Indian History*, University of Oklahoma Press, Norman, 1934, p. 136; "How Good Were Indians as Shooters?" *Guns Magazine*, December, 1956, Vol. II, No. 12-24, pp. 20-23, 74-75.

without understanding of the Indian campaign of which Custer's last fight was a part.

Custer, a youngster just out of West Point, joined his regiment on the battlefield of Bull Run. In the two years following he was commended as staff officer by a curiously diverse list of generals—Phil Kearny, Baldy Smith, Hancock, Barnard, McClellan, Hooker. Alfred Pleasanton, seeking to pep up his Cavalry Corps, jumped Custer from first lieutenant to brigadier general, also naming Captain Elon J. Farnsworth, later killed at Gettysburg, and Captain Wesley Merritt. Pleasanton was ousted for Philip Sheridan, and Sheridan, at the end of the war, endorsed Pleasanton's judgment by picking Merritt and Custer as his division commanders on a mission to the Texas border that might have escalated into war with Emperor Maximilian of Mexico and Emperor Napoleon III of France.

As Civil War brigade and division commander, Custer took one licking (at Lacey's Springs) from his West Point friend and Confederate opponent Thomas J. Rosser. But Custer was in the right place at the right time at Gettysburg, Cold Harbor, Yellow Tavern, Cedar Creek, Waynesboro, and Five Forks, and in at least four of these battles displayed qualities of generalship little to be expected from a youngster in his 24th to 26th years of age.

Custer was an ideal 19th century hero—in a day when there was such a thing as an ideal, and such a thing as a hero. He did not smoke. He quit drinking in 1861 with all the fervor of a dedicated member of Alcoholics Anonymous. He was, presumably, good to his mother. He played rude, practical jokes on his father. He was a devoted husband. He had an adoring wife, of gentle breeding, as would have been said then, who allowed no frontier hardships to deter her from accompanying him to any post of duty where her presence would be permitted.

Custer was a fighting man in an age of fighting men. He was also egocentric, egotistic, and theatrical—and at times a detestable show-off. He had many of the qualities that made General George Patton so controversial in a later war and, like Patton, Custer had a genius for blundering into unnecessary trouble. Detractors have vastly exaggerated the importance of some of this blundering. The "boy general" is an easy target, but why so many writers put so much venom in their target-shooting is a continuing mystery.

Typically Custer put his foot in his mouth just before Little Big Horn. He was overheard and called before a congressional committee to tell what he knew about irregularities in army-post traderships. All Custer could tell was hearsay, but some of that hearsay reflected upon President Grant's friend, Secretary of War Belknap. Custer found difficulty in getting out of this Washington entanglement. When he took off to join the expedition against the Sioux, Grant had him stopped and placed in arrest. Eventually the President relented and allowed Custer to serve with his regiment as lieutenant colonel, but not as commander of the expedition as had been intended, presumably in his rank as brevet major general. The Department of Dakota commander, Brigadier General Alfred H. Terry, led the expedition.

The objective was a band or bands of hostile Sioux headed by Sitting Bull and Crazy Horse, who had never signed a treaty, and had refused to go on a reservation. Their numbers were unknown, but for two years the Indian Bureau had reported that they were incapable of mustering more than 500 warriors for any one fight. Two other expeditions moved against them. One, from the other end of Terry's department in Montana Territory was commanded by Brevet Major General John Gibbon, colonel of the 7th Infantry. It moved eastward toward Terry. From the south came a column commanded by Brigadier General George Crook of the Department of the Platte. "As no very correct information can be obtained as to the location of the hostile Indians, and as there would be no telling how long they would stay at any one place if it were known," said General Sheridan, he did not order the columns to converge on any one area, but rather planned that the wide encirclement would push the Indians toward the reservations.

Terry's column left Fort Abraham Lincoln, Dakota Territory, May 17, 1876, and by June 10 had seen no Indians. On that date Major Marcus A. Reno was sent on a scout with half the 7th Cavalry along the Powder and Tongue Rivers. He picked up a trail of warriors—estimated at about 800— and followed it to the Rosebud. He turned back, not knowing of course that on the same day General Crook was unsuccessfully fighting the great mass of Indians farther up the same stream.

Custer was critical of Reno for not continuing to follow the trail of the Indians. This makes it evident that Custer would have followed such a trail vigorously once he found it. Much of the argument over whether Custer disobeyed Terry's order revolves about this point. Terry and Gibbon had joined forces, and Gibbon was to cross the Yellowstone River and move up the Big Horn to the Little Big Horn, while Custer with the entire 7th Cavalry was to follow the trail seen by Reno. Afterward this seemed a more perfect plan to surround the Indians than it did at the time, when it was not known that the Indians would be found where Custer found them.

The primary error was underestimating the numbers of the Indians. Instead of the expected 500 to 1,000 warriors there was a huge village afterward guessed at 5,000 or 9,000 or even 15,000. The lowest guess on fighting men was 2,500, and fewer than that would have been enough. The efforts of Custer, and the orders of Terry and of Sheridan, were directed toward preventing their escape. The mass was too great for escape; the Indians could only stand and fight. It is improbable, as was supposed at the time, that this was a contrived trap for Custer. The assembly was, at least in part, fortuitous. It was a good year for buffalo hunting. Had it not been, so large a village could not have lived for a day.

As Custer followed the trail, there were several circumstances that gave him the impression that he had been discovered by the Indians. Possibly for this reason he speeded his march. When his Crow and Arikara scouts reported the location of the village, Custer divided his force, sending Captain Frederick W. Benteen with three companies to the left while Major Reno with three companies crossed the Little Big Horn and charged the upper end of the village. Custer with five companies continued down the Little Big Horn. One company guarded the mule pack train.

There is much Sioux testimony to indicate that the attack came as a surprise. Had Reno been of a different temperament, he might have pushed his charge successfully, but it was his judgment at the time that this could not be done, and no one can be sure that he was not right. He ordered his men to dismount and fight on foot, and when he saw that he was being surrounded, led a retreat or, as he called it, a charge, to a defensive position on bluffs across the river. Losses were heavy in this move. Benteen, having found no Indians, had turned back and came upon Reno at this time, helping to organize the defense.

Custer's often-quoted last message, carried by Trumpeter John Martin, read: "Benteen. Come on. Big village. Be quick. Bring packs. W. W. Cooke. P.S. Bring pacs." Cooke was Custer's adjutant. By "packs" and the repeated "pacs" he meant the ammunition packs. Martin reached Benteen before the junction with Reno and reported that when he left Custer was about to charge the village.

That is all that is known, but hundreds of writers and artists have recorded their ideas of Custer's last stand. The bodies were found two days later. Their positions told Benteen nothing about how the fight had gone. Others reported them fallen in orderly formations, one company after another overwhelmed by the Sioux and Cheyenne hordes. Even their number is in doubt: 270 were killed in the battle, of which perhaps 212 were with Custer. Dead were Custer, members of his staff, and all of

Companies C, E, F, I, and L. Among them were Custer's brother Thomas, a captain; his brother Boston and his nephew Autie Reed, civilian employes, and his brother-in-law Lieutenant James Calhoun.

The writers and the artists take off from here.

THE PICTURES

News moved slowly in 1876. General Terry sent the scout Muggins Taylor to the nearest telegraph station at Bozeman with dispatches reporting the disaster, but the telegrapher had taken off for the Fourth of July holiday, and the dispatches were sent from Bozeman to Helena by mail coach. The *Bozeman Times*, July 3, and the *Helena Daily Herald*, July 4, got out extras on what they could get out of Muggins Taylor and scooped the nation with the first inaccuracies about the Custer fight. Meanwhile the steamer *Far West* broke Missouri River records in getting the wounded to Bismarck, and C. A. Lounsberry, employer of Mark Kellogg, the correspondent killed with Custer, broke the news to the nation by getting out an extra of the *Bismarck Tribune*, July 6, while J. M. Carnahan telegraphed the entire story "on a Morse key for nearly sixty hours practically continuous" to the *New York Herald*.[6] Both papers carried the casualty list on page one.

Contrary to what you may have seen in close-ups in motion pictures and television, there were no big, black, bold headlines stretching across the tops of metropolitan newspapers in 1876. The customary headline was single column, starting with a single word or short phrase, followed by a series of ten to a dozen pyramided banks and keylines, set apart by dashes. Some of the top heads over the Custer story were MASSACRE, HORRIBLE, A TERRIBLE FIGHT, GREAT BATTLE WITH THE INDIANS. There were no portraits of Custer or of anyone else, no maps—and no pictures.

Newspapers of 1876 were not entirely devoid of pictures. The Republican eagle screamed or the Democratic rooster crowed over election returns. Tiny steamboats, locomotives, horses, carriages, and wagons decorated appropriate advertising, but these were stock cuts, prepared in advance of the occasion for their use. There was no way of illustrating spot news; all available illustrative processes were too time-consuming.

There was a demand for pictures, and it was met in various ways. Photography, available since 1839, was the most accurate, but its product was static; the wet-plate process required long exposure, and there were no snapshots. There are a few photographs of the Mexican War, and hundreds of the Civil War, a few of which may be regarded as showing troops in action. There are none showing troops fighting Indians. An amazing number of news-type photographic prints was sold to the general public. Collections of carte-de-visite – the size of a calling card – portraits of generals were popular, at a cost of 25 cents apiece or less. Custer was available in several poses among the hundred or so photographic portraits taken of him.

But by far the largest sale of original photographic prints of a public interest subject matter came with the application in 1849 of photography to the stereoscope.

That simple instrument, consisting of two eyepieces and a slide-holder to focus the twin photographs, appeared on every parlor table for a half century or so—say from 1865 to 1915—bringing the world into the home as did nothing else until television. You could tour Europe or Yellowstone Park, accompany Custer through the Black Hills, or meet Crook's column coming in from its horsemeat march at the close of the 1876 summer campaign. But there were no stereo views, no photographs of any kind, of any part of the 1876 movements of Terry, Gibbon, or Custer.

Public demand for news pictures was met quite successfully by the weekly illustrated magazines, which were in many ways the equivalent of today's *Time, Life, Newsweek, Look*, and *National Geographic* magazines. The *Illustrated London News* set the pattern in 1842, and *Frank Leslie's Illustrated Newspaper* started in New York in 1855, lasting until 1922. *Harper's Weekly* came along in 1857 and stayed on until 1916. The weeklies made tremendous reputations for their Civil War coverage. Their pictures were wood engravings, the only practicable method then known of reproducing illustrations that could be printed with type in a printing press. In wood engraving, the lines and marks to be printed were in relief and could be inked along with the type. In engraving on copper or steel, the lines and marks were cut into the plate and when printed were filled with ink while the surface was kept clean. Engraving styles were line engraving, including etching; mezzotint, stippling, and aquatint. When used for book illustration, they were separately printed. All were slow and laborious processes.

Wood engraving was slow enough. The wood—boxwood from Turkey was preferred—was cut across the grain in type-height slices. For large illustrations, as many as 50 to 100 blocks of wood might be joined together. The surface was covered with Chinese white, and the picture, perhaps "from a photograph", more commonly from an artist's sketch, was copied in India ink and pencil. The engraver then went to work on the wood with gravers, tint-tools, and scoopers to carve out an illustration in relief. On a rush job, the hundred blocks might be taken apart and each given to an engraver. A rush job might be finished in a couple of weeks.

Thus *Harper's* might—and did—send Winslow Homer to sketch Civil War battlefields, but what showed up in the weekly depended considerably on the art of the engraver. On the other hand, the engraver might vastly improve the work of an inferior artist. It was common to credit both. "Sculpsit", abbreviated *sc.* or *sculp.*, most often in the lower right corner, indicated the engraver. "Pinxit", abbreviated *pxt.* or *pinx.*, designated the painter; if a drawing, *del.* referred to the delineator.

The first picture of Custer's last fight was a woodcut in the *New York Graphic and Illustrated Evening Newspaper* dated July 19, 1876, thirteen days after the earliest telegraphed reports. "The Battle on the Little Big Horn River—The Death Struggle of General Custer" **(plate I)** was drawn, says the caption, by Mr. W. M. Cary "from sketches and description by our special correspondent." It is a crude woodcut, showing evidence of haste, with much use of the cross-hatching despised by Thomas Bewick, the great English woodcut artist who did his own engraving. But it set the pace for all others, closely approximating the much later lithograph so widely distributed by Anheuser-Busch. The picture centers on Custer with one foot resting on a dead horse, saber in his right hand, revolver in his left, broad-brimmed hat, uniform coat, flowing necktie, booted and spurred. Most of this is wrong, notably the sabers all over the place. (There were none.) In the foreground are horses transfixed with arrows, and the inevitable dead troopers. A large array of mounted Indians surrounds the last stand.

William de la Montagne Cary (1840-1922), born in Tappan, New York, however, was peculiarly qualified to become the first Custer fight artist. He had sketched Indians up the Missouri River to Fort Benton as early as 1861. In 1874 he had been with the Northern Boundary Commission, which was escorted by Major Reno's squadron, so he should have known what a 7th Cavalry trooper looked like in the field. Cary's work was used by *Harper's Weekly*, *Leslie's*, *St. Nicholas*, and by Currier & Ives. An able Western illustrator, he was to return again and again to the subject of Custer, although his first last flight was soon forgotten. Another and better version—the engraver Horace Baker signed this one—served through many editions of *Barnes's Brief History of the United States* and its successor *The Story of the Great Republic*, as well as *Barnes's New National*

16

Plate I. William de la Montagne Cary
The Battle of the Little Big Horn River — The Death Struggle of General Custer, 1876
From *New York Graphic Illustrated Newspaper*, July 19, 1876
Courtesy of The Library of Congress

Fifth Reader and even John Clark Ridpath's *History of the World*. Another Cary composition, "Custer's Last Ride," appeared in Volume IX of *The Story of the Greatest Nations* by the able and prolific dime-novelist and historian Edward S. Ellis, in collaboration with Charles F. Horne (1913). Cary was at his best—or longest remembered—in his illustrations for the juvenile *The Master of the Strong Hearts, A Story of Custer's Last Rally*, by Elbridge S. Brooks, published in 1898 and reprinted as late as 1925.[2]

The short-lived *New York Graphic* beat *Harper's Weekly* by ten days. *Harper's* coverage of Custer was weak pictorially, consisting of illustrations by C. S. Reinhart on July 29, 1876, for a set of verses called "Romance and Reality." One of the two panels, "Romance on the Hudson" shows a cadet at West Point; the other, "Reality on the Plains," shows the cadet dead on a battlefield, presumably the Little Big Horn. It comes close to being an editorial cartoon. Frederick Opper, later famed as the creator of Happy Hooligan and illustrator of Bill Nye's *Comic History of the United States*, was deadly serious in his 1876 editorial cartoon depicting a vicious-looking Sitting Bull holding scalps of the Custer family under a heading, "His hour of triumph; but how long will it last?"

The first book illustration of "Custer's Last Fight," and one of the most frequently reproduced, came of course in Frederick Whittaker's *A Complete Life of Gen. George A. Custer*, rushed into print in 1876. The artist, appropriately, was Alfred R. Waud, who had contributed to Custer's early fame with many sketches in *Harper's Weekly*, who had accompanied as artist and correspondent Custer's raid in March, 1864, across the Rapidan, and who had done some of the illustrations for Custer's *My Life on the Plains*. Waud, rated by the Library of Congress as "one of the most important illustrators of American history," was born in London, England, in 1828. Coming to New York in 1858 he exhibited at the National Academy of Design, but gained his greatest fame for his work in *Harper's Weekly* during the Civil War. His brother William Waud served *Leslie's* in a similar capacity during the Seven Days' Battles and later worked with Alfred for *Harper's*. In 1866 Alfred Waud sketched post-war New Orleans for *Harper's Weekly*; in 1871 he covered the Chicago Fire for *Every Saturday*; he did many sketches for *Battles and Leaders of the Civil War* for *Century*. Waud died in 1891 in Marietta, Georgia, while on a sketching tour of battlefields in the South. The Library of Congress critic says Waud "employed a quick, light touch, an impressionism, and even a shorthand which are thoroughly modern." Waud's original pencil and wash drawings fared ill at the hands of the wood engravers.[3]

Waud's composition centers on a standing, buckskin-clad Custer, firing a revolver, a rifle in his other hand; three men still firing around him; three more dying at his feet, as Indians, afoot and on horseback, close in from the background. It is a spirited drawing lacking the gruesomeness of many others—although Waud did not always forego realism, as his sketch of the Kidder massacre testifies. The engraving signed "McCracken" in the Whittaker biography is by far the best of many reproductions and treatments of Waud's Custer fight. An engraving signed "Williams" in W. Fletcher Johnson's *Life of Sitting Bull* is much scratchier and less finished.

Another "Custer's Last Stand" by Waud probably was first used in 1892 in *Indian Wars of the United States*, another of the many histories by Edward S. Ellis. It is of somewhat similar composition, although vertical rather than horizontal, giving more impression of the Last Stand hill—and a dead horse to extend the foreground.

Both Waud concepts have been widely copied, re-engraved, and consciously imitated. An example is an oil painting **(plate II)** attributed to Waud, but more likely the work of a primitive artist who used the Waud drawing as his model.

Another artist who is said to have worked for *Leslie's* and *Harper's* was George Henry Ellsbury (1840-1900). A Civil War veteran who fought in the Sioux War in Minnesota in 1862 with Company D, 7th Minnesota Infantry, he gathered material on the battlefield and from Indian survivors for his "Custer's Last Battle," painted in 1887 **(plate III).** It is not known to have been used for any illustrative purpose.

Public demand for news pictures was also met by the large lithographs, suitable for framing, often in color. They were printed on sheets of paper from 28 by 40 inches down to 13 by 17. The printing was done from a flat stone—a pearl-gray limestone from Bavaria was preferred—on which a drawing was copied with grease crayon. After etching with nitric acid and gum arabic, the stone was moistened. The wet parts repelled ink, so that only the parts drawn received ink for printing.

These large lithographs are commonly associated with the firm of Currier & Ives; they produced more over a longer period, and they were always—well, nearly always—hot on the news. In 1835, Nathaniel Currier went into business with prints of spectacular fires at the Planters Hotel in New Orleans and the Merchant's Exchange in New York. In 1857 he took on James Merritt Ives as partner. The Civil War boomed their business—every soldier and sailor wanted a print of the battle he had fought to send to the folks back home.[4]

Chromolithographs—lithographs printed in color—are almost as old as

Plate II. Artist Unknown
Custer's Last Stand
Oil, 28½ by 54½ inches, date unknown
Courtesy of Mr. James R. Meyer, Hastings, Minnesota

Plate III. Colonel George Henry Ellsbury
Custer's Last Battle
Oil, 46 x 70 inches, 1887
Courtesy of Mr. H. S. Ellsbury and The Shorey Book Store, Seattle, Washington

the lithographic process itself, but required a separate stone for each color used, and getting several drawings in register proved difficult until photography came to the rescue. "Chromo" became a byword for a crudely done, garishly colored illustration. "Death of General Custer" in J. W. Buel's *Heroes of the Plains* (1883) is a peculiarly horrible example, not quite matched by a frontispiece, "Custer's Last Rally on the Little Big Horn", in D. M. Kelsey's *Our Pioneer Heroes and Their Daring Deeds* (1882).

Currier & Ives preferred hand coloring on a production-line basis, each worker putting on one color. Despite all this labor, costs were not high. Currier & Ives farmed out one batch of 2,378 assorted pictures to James Baillie for coloring, and the bill came to one cent a print. Lithographs sold for 25 cents or less, depending on size and subject matter.[5] Many were used as supplements to newspapers, and this continued into the 20th century. An example is Edgar Cameron's "Custer's Fight" **(plate IV)** printed by the American Colortype Company and issued as a supplement to the *St. Louis Globe Democrat* of May 4, 1902.

Currier & Ives flunked out completely on the Little Big Horn. They did not come off second best; it would be a tight squeeze to rate them eight-hundredth best. There was a "Custer's Last Charge," copyright 1876 by Currier & Ives. All it showed was Custer in a blue uniform, faced in red, waving a saber, galloping off on a worried-looking white horse. The anachronisms were no oversight; it was a quick makeover of a Civil War picture. Union soldiers were wiped out—but Custer retained a brigadier general's shoulder straps, which he had not worn since 1864. But how were Mr. Currier and Mr. Ives to know that "Custer's Last Fight" was to become the most popular lithographic subject of all time?

The first classic color lithograph of the Little Big Horn was done in 1876 by the Milwaukee Lithographing and Engraving Company and entered for copyright by Seifert Gugler & Co. It also was titled "Custer's Last Charge," with the subtitle "Custer's Todes-Ritt" **(plate V)** for the producer's German trade. Again Custer is in full uniform, waving a saber, but he has switched to a dark horse, and the saber is about to come down on a mounted Indian armed only with a coup stick. At this stage of the action, it looks bad for the Indians: one lies dead in dead-center fore-ground; another, just behind, has thrown up his hands in mortal agony; and a third is running headlong toward the lower right corner. The picture is full of mounted soldiers and Indians moving in several directions, the hills in background are not out of character for the area, and considering how little was known then—or since—about what actually happened, it is

22

Plate IV. Edgar Cameron
Custer's Fight — Little Big Horn River — June 25, 1876
Lithograph, 8¼x10¾ inches, 1902
Amon Carter Museum Collection

Plate V. Feodor Fuchs
Custer's Last Charge
Lithograph, 21½ x 26⅞ inches, ca. 1876
Courtesy of The Library of Congress

not too bad a composition of what might have been. The artist was Feodor Fuchs, who sometimes anglicized his first name as Theodore. In 1856 his address was 17 Minor Street, Philadelphia; he did frontispieces for the *Horticulturist and Journal of Rural Art and Rural Taste* and portraits of Civil War personages, including the German-American hero Major General Franz Sigel—popularized during the war by a quasi-humorous poem, "I fights mit Sigel."

It was not until March, 1878, that the Pacific Art Company of San Francisco copyrighted the lithograph "General Custer's Death Struggle," which proved one of the most popular, perhaps because it is so atrociously bad. A savage-looking Custer, again in dress uniform, again swings a saber, with one foot on a dead horse, a white horse this time. His mounted Indian opponent, however, has already fired a revolver, so that the end of the death struggle must be only split seconds away. Custer is surrounded by hand-to-hand conflicts and scalpings, while grotesquely savage warriors wield wicked-looking warclubs and tomahawks. In background a mounted Indian makes off with a captured Stars and Stripes that does not appear to be one of the guidons actually there. More sabers, and mountains of near-Bierstadt proportions are added anachronisms. The work is signed H. Steinegger and the credit "S. H. Redmond del" presumably means that Redmond delineated it for the lithograph. The lithographer was Britton Rey & Co.

There is not much more that can be regarded as contemporary. A primitive—and the classification is apt—by W. J. Wallack of Nebraska is attributed to 1876. An equally primitive woodcut was drawn by one Kelly and engraved by J. I. Engling in 1878 for "Tic Tacs" by the Homer Lee Bank-Note Co., and reproduced in the 1886 edition of Captain Jack Crawford's *The Poet Scout.*

Whether any of the numerous depictions of the fight from the Indian side can be dated to 1876 is doubtful; most of them were not discovered until years later. That the subject was a popular one among the victors is proved by numbers, including three lengthy series of pictures by as many artists. They are done in a wide variety of mediums, in pencil, in water color, and oil, on buffalo hide, deerskin, cowhide, cotton sheeting, wrapping paper, old ledgers, and discarded books of army forms. Most of them are symbolic and, like the many stories told by Indian participants, add little to our information about the fight—yet sometimes they can reach through to an alien and barbaric point of view and help to interpret the Sioux and Cheyenne way of looking at their world.

Earliest, most extensive, and perhaps most useful are those of Red Horse, a Sioux, reported in the *Tenth Annual Report of the Bureau of Ethnology*, 1888-'89, as gathered by Dr. Charles E. McChesney, acting assistant surgeon, U. S. Army, consisting of 41 sheets of manila paper, averaging 24 by 36 inches, accompanied by a map, which is dated 1881, and a narrative. The report reproduces nine of the drawings, three in color, omitting the rest on the ground that "they are made objectionable by monotonous repetitions." A striking one is that titled "Custer's Dead Cavalry" showing that Indians had no compunction about depicting the ritualistic dismembering of bodies—and indicating that Red Horse's art was not guided by the white man's ideas. (Another variation is shown in **plate VI.**)

Another of early date, but admittedly done to order, is that of Little Big Man, or Tanka Cical Wacasa, reproduced in W. Fletcher Johnson's *Life of Sitting Bull*, 1891. Thomas B. Marquis obtained three from Wooden Leg and one from Big Beaver, but did not use them in his publications. John G. Neihardt used two by Standing Bear in *Black Elk Speaks*. Stanley Vestal sponsored two by Joseph White Bull. Of interest are the painting by Kicking Bear in the Southwest Museum, the drawing by White Bird, a Northern Cheyenne, in the United States Military Academy, the deer-skin decorated by a Northern Cheyenne and the sheet by an Oglala Sioux in the Museum of the American Indian, and the canvas by One Bull. Father Peter John Powell recently turned up a series of brightly done water colors painted on the ruled pages of a ledger by a Cheyenne scout, including eleven relating to the Little Big Horn. Perhaps the most elaborately reproduced are those of Amos Bad Heart Buffalo and Kills Two **(plate VII)** in a portfolio of colored plates published in Nice, France, in 1938. Sixteen plates relate to the Little Big Horn. At another angle is the work of the Indian illustrator Brumett Echohawk, a Pawnee, who has also turned his hand to Custer fight pictures.

One business based on the 19th century public's insatiable demand for pictures that awes a generation of television viewers is the reproduction of paintings as a branch of show business. In our time paintings are restricted to art galleries and museums; if admission is charged, we donate our fee, culture-conscious, to see Art with a capital A—and if we are way-out culture-conscious, we do not expect to see pictures. It just does not seem possible that anything that could be dubbed oil-on-canvas could be hawked around as a tent show, competing with glass blowers, Adam Forepaugh's Circus, Swiss bell ringers, the (old) Christy's Minstrels, *Uncle*

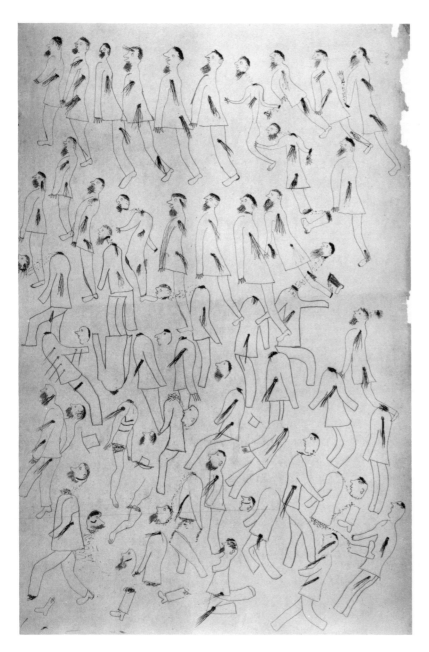

Plate VI. Red Horse
Dead Cavalry — Custer's Column
Drawing, 36x24 inches, 1881
Courtesy of The Smithsonian Institution, Office of Anthropology

Tom's Cabin, burlesque, Buffalo Bill's Wild West, *The Black Crook*, (denounced for its flagrant indecency), medicine shows, *Ben-Hur*, (with chariot race on stage, live), ventriloquists, hypnotists, or Joseph Jefferson as *Rip Van Winkle*.

If it could be done at all, the Custer fight might be expected to have some of the curiosity appeal of the Siamese Twins, the long hair of the Seven Sutherland Sisters, the shortness of the midgets Tom Thumb and "Commodore Foote," and the Eden Musée and Chamber of Horrors.

First to see its possibilities was John Mulvany (1844-1906). Born in Ireland, Mulvany came to New York at 12 years of age and picked up some skills at drawing and sketching while working at the Academy of Design. After service in the Civil War, he went abroad and studied art under such painters of battle-pieces as Piloty and Wagner in Munich and De Keyser in Antwerp. In 1876, Mulvany exhibited a Western subject, "The Preliminary Trial of a Horse Thief" at the National Academy of Design. He was living in Kansas City in 1879 when he began work on his Custer fight picture, visiting the battlefield, the Sioux reservations, and Fort Leavenworth in his search for authentic detail. He took the picture to Boston in April, 1881, and made some changes suggested by critics. Edward Clements of the *Boston Transcript* praised it as "an original and American composition" in contrast to "conventional battle-pieces of European art," finding it "real, not only in its vigor and desperation, but in fidelity to the facts of modern and contemporary American fighting ... a grim, dismal mêlée."

"Custer's Last Rally," as Mulvany called it, was a huge painting, 11x22 feet, its foreground figures in heroic size. Custer is short-haired, wears a lapeled uniform coat, fires a revolver, and holds the inevitable saber. It was first exhibited in New York City in the summer of 1881, where it was greeted with enthusiasm by Walt Whitman as sketched "from reality, or the best that could be got of it" and "painfully real, overwhelming, needs good nerves to look at it.... There is almost entire absence of the stock traits of European war pictures; ... one of the very few attempts at deliberate artistic expression for our land and people, on a pretty ambitious standard and programme, that impressed me as filling the bill."

The emphasis on realism may jar modernists, but when one recalls the Grecian urns and Roman columns, the prettiness and imitativeness of much American painting of the time, Mulvany may have moved out quite a bit.

"Custer's Last Rally" was exhibited by the Polytechnic Society in Louisville in December, 1881, and was shown in Chicago in 1882 and again in 1890. A pamphlet of "Press Comments" was issued in Chicago. A small copy of the painting, 34½ by 18½ inches, was made by Mulvany for production of the color lithograph, which measures almost exactly the same size—lithographers could not work from a 20-foot-long canvas. The lithograph was produced by the Chicago Lithograph and Engraving Company, which claimed copyright, but neglected to give it a date; 1881 seems probable. The credits are "Jno. Mulvany, pinxt." which means he painted it, and "D. C. Fabronius, del" which means that he redrew it for the lithographic stone. A small, black-and-white lithograph, one of those handsome jobs on heavy paper, was done as frontispiece for John F. Finerty's *War-Path and Bivouac* in 1890—apparently in small numbers, as some even of the original printings, and most of the reprints seem not to have it. Reproductions, of which there have been many, may come from any one of the four—two paintings and two lithographs—each of which varies slightly, as all were done by hand.

Mulvany painted other pictures—"The Scouts of the Yellowstone" and "Sunrise on the Rocky Mountains," other battle pictures, "Sheridan's Ride from Winchester," "McPherson and Revenge" or "The Battle of Atlanta," or both, and "An Incident of the Boer War," portraits of John C. Breckenridge and Henry Watterson, and even something called "Love's Mirror" or "Venus at the Bath." He is remembered, if at all, for "Custer's Last Rally," which is said to have made him "a small fortune." In 1906 he drowned himself in the East River.[6]

Another early lithograph, contemporary with Mulvany's, was "The Last Battle of General Custer," **(plate VIII)** copyrighted by H. Bencke in 1882.

The "Custer's Last Fight" that everyone remembers is a lithograph sometimes bearing the legend, "The original painting by Cassilly Adams has been presented to The Seventh Regiment U. S. Cavalry by Mr. Adolphus Busch." Few Americans have missed seeing one of the 150,000 copies of this work, distributed for a half century and more, by Anheuser-Busch. You could see it for free, with your nickel beer while eating your free lunch in almost any saloon. However it bore only casual resemblance to the show-piece painted by Cassilly Adams to be exhibited at 50 cents admission.

Cassilly Adams was born in Zanesville, Ohio, July 18, 1843, the son of William Apthorp Adams and Mary Biddle Cassilly Adams. A student in Cincinnati when Confederate General Kirby Smith threatened that city, Cassilly Adams volunteered for thirty days in the militia, serving in Captain Russel's company, called the Scott Rifles, of Colonel Robinson's regiment. "We were marched over the Ohio River on pontoons and thrown

Copyrighted by H Bencke 1882.

The Last Battle of Gen Custer

Plate VIII. H. Bencke
The Last Battle of General Custer
Lithograph, 24⅛x29-9/16 inches, 1882
Courtesy of The Library of Congress

into the rifle pits on the Kentucky hills" under orders of Major General Lew. Wallace, Cassilly Adams recorded. He enlisted in the Navy on December 16, 1862, serving in the Mississippi Squadron as master's mate and acting ensign on the *Linden, Osage,* and *Ouachita.* His painting of the *Osage,* a single-turret monitor, was presented to the U. S. Naval Academy Museum in 1961. Adams was discharged in Cincinnati on September 15, 1865, lived there until 1878, in St. Louis until 1886, Cincinnati until 1889, Toledo until 1908, Detroit until 1910, and then Indianapolis, where he died on May 8, 1921. A fragmentary list of his work includes sketches of a banjo player and other sketches made while recuperating from yellow fever in Louisiana, and pen-and-ink for a wood engraving called "Trip to Arcadia," a pencil sketch of Doc Middleton, the Nebraska bandit, and paintings called "Nude" and "Dead Squaw on the Prairie." If further identification is required, Cassilly Adams described himself at age 62 as: occupation, artist; height, 5 feet, 11 inches; weight, 159 pounds; blue eyes, gray hair, light complexion, blue dot tattooed on left forearm. This array of facts may serve to show that Cassilly Adams was no mythological character.[7]

"Custer's Last Fight" **(plate IX)** was painted during his residence in St. Louis between 1878 and 1886. A faded invitation to a studio warming in Room 52, fifth floor, southeast corner of Fifth and Olive streets, seems to be dated February, 1884, and his partner's name appears to be T. or T. T. Richards, presumably the T. Richards who with C. J. Budd financed the picture in hope of great returns. Ticket seller and barker for the show was Billy Fox, whose sister Della Fox was a famous stage soubrette. They were neighbors of Cassilly Adams in St. Louis.

The earliest date that can be attached to the picture is April 26, 1886, when copyright No. 9562 was issued to John G. Furber covering a four-page printed pamphlet descriptive of *Custer's Last Fight. Painted by Cassilly Adams. Representing the Last Grand Indian Battle that will ever be fought on this Continent. 12 feet high by 32 feet long, valued at $50,000.* To this was attached a photographic copy of the painting. Who was John G. Furber? St. Louis directories of 1885 to 1888 show that John G. Furber operated a saloon at 724, or 726, Olive Street. He must have bought in for a corner of the show.

Forty-eight years later verifiable data indicate that the picture had shrunk from 12 by 32 feet to 9 feet, 6 inches, by 16 feet, 5 inches. The missing two-and-one-half feet of height could have been a faked strip of sky

32

Plate IX. Cassilly Adams
Custer's Last Fight
Oil on canvas, 113x197 inches, 1886
Courtesy of The Library of Congress

added for exhibition purposes. The missing width is accounted for in the pamphlet's description of two side pieces:

> The picture on the right entitled "Coming Events Cast their Shadows Before" illustrated an episode in childhood days of Custer. His father, who was a member of the "New Rumley Invincibles," took great pride in teaching his little son the manual of arms according to Scott's tactics, as here represented, "Shoulder Arms!"

> The picture to the left, entitled, "Revered even by his Savage Foes," shows the reverence the Indians must have had for Custer. Every other body was stripped, scalped and most horribly mutilated, but propped in the position here represented they found him. The figure laying [sic] across his feet has his throat cut; that is the mark of the Sioux; they are known among the Indians as the cut-throats. The shooting of arrows into a corpse also denoted that the owner of the arrows did it. An Indian's arrows are feathered and marked alike, so that he and surrounding bands know them.

The copyright date indicates that the show was on the road in 1886. Cassilly Adams says he moved from St. Louis to Cincinnati in 1886. It is generally agreed that the tour was no great success, and that the picture was brought back to St. Louis. *The Kansas City Gazette* reported in 1903 that the painting hung in a saloon at Eighth and Olive streets, and that the saloon's owner died in 1888, which checks with the data on Furber. The story continues that the saloon owner's brother took over, and went into bankruptcy two years later, whereupon the picture was seized as a creditor's asset by Anheuser-Busch, which checks with that firm's 1890 date for its acquisition. Another story is that the exhibitors sold the picture, valued in their publicity at $50,000, to Adolphus Busch for $30,000. This may mean that Adolphus Busch settled the claims of Richards and Budd. Presumably Adams was out of it, as he is said to have opposed the use of his painting for beer advertising.

Publicity for Anheuser-Busch, Inc., formerly the Anheuser-Busch Brewing Association, says that the painting was presented to the 7th Cavalry in 1890, but it seems unlikely that the gift was made before the lithograph was produced. The War Department in its 1920 inquiry used the date 1895, and this checks out. Regimental tradition agrees that it was while the 7th was stationed at Fort Riley, Kansas, which would be between 1888 and 1895, and that when the 7th was transferred to Fort Grant, Arizona, the painting was taken along in a yellow-painted box, 10 feet long by

2 feet square. When the 7th left Fort Grant for Cuba in 1898, the painting was left behind. Years later, Carl S. Gung'l, caretaker of the post, found the two side panels and stored them at his ranch nearby. In 1944, his son gave the two panels to the Arizona Pioneers' Historical Society, but without the proper documentation. It was not until recently that they were identified as the missing side panels to Adams' painting.

In 1921, as a result of the War Department inquiry, the large center canvas was reported in storage with 7th Cavalry property at Fort Bliss, Texas. After Colonel John K. Herr, later major general, last chief of cavalry, and cavalry historian, took command of the regiment in 1935, he had the canvas unrolled, and found it badly cracked and damaged. Painters whom he consulted estimated restoration would cost from $10,000 to $18,000, so Colonel Herr turned to the WPA. Its art division in Boston, Massachusetts, agreed to do the job—the cost was $4,218—on condition that the WPA be allowed to exhibit the painting in Boston for six months. In 1938 it was returned to the 7th Cavalry at Fort Bliss and displayed at the consolidated officers' mess. To find room, it was necessary to tear out one wall. According to Captain Edward S. Luce, one of a committee put in charge by Colonel William W. West, a new wall was built of vitrified brick; the painting was roped to a zinc-copper plate as backing, and put behind "fireproof" glass. A fire in the officers' mess on June 13, 1946, destroyed the painting. Thus ends the story of "Custer's Last Fight" as painted by Cassilly Adams.[8]

But what of the 150,000 lithographs distributed to saloons? In the days of stone lithography it was expedient to have a large painting copied to a size near that wanted for the print, as Mulvany had done with his large painting. F. Otto Becker of Milwaukee was employed in 1895 to paint the version used; according to Mr. Becker, "This work was obtained by the Milwaukee Lithographing Company through Mr. Arthur Koenig, a personal friend of Mr. Adolphus Busch." Becker's painting was cut into eight or more pieces, so that a number of artists could work on it at the same time in making the color plates. In 1936 Roland F. Becker, son of the artist, had the sections mounted on a piece of masonite, and his father painted over the seams, and as the cuts had not gone into or through any of the figures, the painting was restored to its original condition. The restored painting was purchased by Anheuser-Busch, Inc. in 1939.[9]

Most copies bear the legend: "Entered according to act of Congress by Adolphus Busch March 30th 1896 in the Office of the Librarian of Congress at Washington, D.C." This sets the date for the beginning of the famous lithograph. Over the years there have been a considerable number of variant printings. Collectors have not determined which came first. Considering the number issued, copies are surprisingly scarce, and collectors are lucky to have one of any printing. They were issued in frames and in some versions, including one of the latest ones, the picture comes to the edge of the frame. Others had wide margins, with space below for identification of some of the figures, the title, presentation, and other data, flanked by an improvised 7th Cavalry coat-of-arms and a representation of the battle monument. The Kansas State Historical Society displays a copy bearing no reference to Anheuser-Busch, Inc., or to that firm's product. This is an intentional deletion and came about after Blanche Boies, a disciple of Carrie Nation, on January 9, 1904, took an axe to the brewing association's publicity, as then displayed in the state museum.

Some lithographs show clearly the signature "O. Becker" and perhaps deservedly, for Becker, although following the main lines of the Cassilly Adams painting, and repeating some features almost identically, made so many changes and additions that it may almost be regarded as a new composition. Some of the changes may have been intended to correct errors to which objection had been made. In the Adams pamphlet "Rain-in-the-Face, seeing the fate of three braves, raises his pistol and fires," killing Custer. In Becker, the Indian is still firing his pistol, but another Indian is identified as Rain-in-the-Face. Adams, depicting the sword-play described by Whittaker, shows Custer with arm outthrust, his saber piercing an Indian standing erect, with tomahawk in his raised hand. Becker's Custer holds the saber over his head and the Indian is tumbling backward. Adams has a steep hill in the background; Becker shows the Little Big Horn valley, with many mounted Indians riding to the attack. Becker has added more figures, including the detailed scalping in center foreground, but Adams is not devoid of this kind of realism.

Anheuser-Busch made other lithographs of historic subjects—but did anyone remember them after fourteen years of Prohibition? Of course not. But customers could not be expected to cry over their Budweiser without looking at "Custer's Last Fight," so the lithograph was reissued. Cassilly Adams spent a lifetime as an able professional artist, but was made famous by the picture he did not paint. As for F. Otto Becker, his masterpiece has been attributed to Remington. That should be glory enough for any lithographer.

Another large painting that was taken on an exhibition tour was that of Edgar Samuel Paxson (1852-1919). Paxson was born in East Hamburg, near Buffalo, New York. His father was a carriage- and sign-painter, and he grew up in that business. When he was 23 he started west, arriving in Montana Territory in 1876, the year of the Custer fight. He worked on cattle ranches and as a guard on stage coaches; he served in the militia during the Nez Percé War. He is said to have visited the Custer battlefield in 1877. In 1879 he sent for his wife and and son and settled down at Deer Lodge, where he started painting—sign painting, house painting, scenery for theaters, murals for saloons, and even portraits of Indians and Western scenes. He sketched incessantly, and eventually was recognized as a top Western artist. He spent 20 years on the painting he preferred to call "Custer's Last Stand," according to his grandson, William Edgar Paxson. He completed it in 1899 after returning from service in the Philippines during the Spanish-American War.

On December 11, 1899, Paxson signed an agreement with William S. Brackett of Peoria, Illinois, for exhibition of the picture for one year on a rental basis. It was shown in Chicago, New York, and Washington, and probably in Philadelphia and other cities. The descriptive pamphlet called it "Custer's Last Battle on the Little Big Horn." It was a huge exhibition painting, 6 x 10 feet. It shows a large number of soldiers and Indians—more than 200 in seething action, is the claim. Many notable Indians are said to have posed for the painting, including Sitting Bull, Gall, Two Moon, Rain-in-the-Face, Nag-s-shaw, Tendoy, and Louison. Although several times reproduced in both black and white and in color, it was not until 1963 that a lithograph, 18¾ by 27 inches, was printed.

Included in the exhibition was a number of smaller paintings by Paxson, which were offered for sale. Whether the promoter profited from the tour does not appear, but it brought Paxson wide recognition. He was commissioned to illustrate a number of books and pamphlets, and his work was reproduced in prints, calendars, and post cards. Among the books was *Life of Reverend L. B. Stateler, A Story of Life on the Old Frontier*, by Rev. E. J. Stanley, published by the Methodist book house in Nashville in 1900, in which one of the illustrations was another version of "Custer's Last Battle."[10]

The huge show-pictures of Cassilly Adams, 12 x 32 feet, Mulvany, 11 x 22 feet, and Paxson, 6 x 10 feet, were dwarfed by another form of exhibition art, the cyclorama, which reached a peak of popularity in the 1880s. This form of art was a development of the panorama, an almost endless picture mounted on two rollers, so that only a section was seen at a time, usually with accompanying lecture. A panorama of the Mississippi Valley was advertised as 15,000 feet long. The cyclorama was not a moving picture, but it was endless; as its name indicates, it was painted in a circle. The viewer found himself in the middle of the scene depicted; sometimes the effect was enhanced by extending the picture with actual objects to the point of viewing. In "The Battle of Atlanta," handsomely preserved in its own building by the City of Atlanta, actual steel rails extend the railroad shown in the painting.

The Franco-Prussian War gave a boost to the cyclorama idea. Paul Philippoteaux won considerable success in Paris with "The Defense of Fort d'Issy," painted in 1871, but soon French and German artists foresaw an even more receptive audience among Civil War veterans and came flocking to America. Philippoteaux painted two of Gettysburg, the smaller of which is still on view at the battlefield. Manassas, Shiloh, Vicksburg, Missionary Ridge, Lookout Mountain, and the Monitor and the Merrimack were other Civil War conflicts celebrated; there was even a third of Gettysburg. Because they were traded around in various cities, they became standardized at about 400 feet circumference. Heights were more flexible, ranging from 27 to 70 feet. Most buildings housing them were of a temporary character, but Chicago, long successful in this type of entertainment, had a structure that served as a theater for many years after the cyclorama craze had ended.

Some thirty-six of these monster paintings could be named. Not all were Civil War battles; other subjects were "Christ's Entry into Jerusalem," "Niagara Falls," "The Chicago Fire," and such late comers as the Spanish-American War battles of Manila and Santiago. Perhaps the last ever to be painted was the "Pantheon de la Guerre," celebrating World War I and said to contain 6,000 portraits of leaders and heroes. It was shown at Chicago's A Century of Progress Exposition in 1933, as was one of the Gettysburgs. Both were found abandoned in warehouses years later.

Of course there was a *Cyclorama of Custer's Last Fight.* It was painted for the Boston Cyclorama Company in 1888 by E. Pierpont and staff, the staff including M. M. Salvador-Mage, Ernest Gros, and Emile Merlot for landscape; Charles A. Corwin, Theo. Wendall, and G. A. Trevers for foreground figures; and E. J. Austin for distant figures and the Indian village. The painting was displayed in Boston in 1889, when a 20-page descriptive booklet was issued with keyed diagram. Mrs. Custer was a consultant on the pamphlet. The cyclorama was afterward shown in Detroit, probably in Chicago, and was last owned in Hollywood. The Library of Congress has a series of photographs showing the cyclorama in ten sections. And that is about all that is known of it.

As may be noted, the assembly-line techniques used in coloring lithographs had been adapted, in large scale, to cyclorama painting. It was a highly specialized occupation. Richard Lorenz (1858-1915) came from Weimar, Germany, in 1886, to Milwaukee to paint horses for the huge show-pictures being created by William Wehner. However, Lorenz was sent to Atlanta, where a 40-foot tower had been erected as hub of the scene that was to be depicted in the cyclorama of "The Battle of Atlanta" and Lorenz sketched the landscape. Technical director was Theodore R. Davis, artist-correspondent who not only had witnessed the battle of Atlanta with Sherman, but had also ridden the Western Plains with Custer—and had spoken kindly of Custer. It may be coincidence, but shortly afterward Lorenz went west, and gained quite a reputation as a Western painter, although he spent most of his life in Milwaukee doing horse-and-buggy scenes. His Custer's Last Stand was called "The Last Glow of a Passing Nation," **(plate X)** is dated 1914, and is 53 by 73 inches (not feet) in size, somewhat short of cyclorama proportions.[11]

As Lorenz had discovered, the day of the show-business picture was coming to an end with the 1880s. The machine age was catching up with art. One trend is seen in the often reproduced "Battle of the Big Horn," by Kurz & Allison, Art Publishers, Chicago, 1889. This was chromolithography to which no one signed a *sculpsit*, *pinxit*, or *del*. It was deservedly anonymous—and it will be noted the unknown perpetrators even blundered the name of the fight. Kurz & Allison did a vast number of Civil War battles of similar quality until "chromo" became a symbol for garish illustration.

The half-tone and other methods of photoengraving came into use about 1890. The fact is strikingly shown in two editions of that curious subscription book, *Wild Life on the Plains*. The 1883 edition by Sun Publishing Company of St. Louis names Custer as author because his book is reprinted—with its original woodcut illustrations, including those by Waud. In the book's added "Horrors of Indian Warfare" is a hodge-podge of anonymous chapters on Little Big Horn, other Indian wars, and heroes of the Plains, all illustrated with woodcuts of inferior quality. The 1891 edition by Royal Publishing Company of St. Louis omits Custer's name as author, and is sometimes attributed to W. L. Holloway, who copyrighted it. He probably had as much to do with writing it as the Olive Street saloon owner had to do with painting the "Custer's Last Fight" that he copyrighted for Cassilly Adams. The only new writing added is two chapters about the Ghost Dance troubles, with some 30 illustrations reproduced

Plate X. Richard Lorenz
The Last Glow of a Passing Nation
Oil on canvas, 53 x 73 inches, 1914
Collection of Mrs. Gunder Torstenson, Moline, Illinois

by the new methods, including a dozen or so modern-type half-tones—crude, but definitely screened half-tones.

These arts developed rapidly, ushering in what might be called the era of the great illustrators, extending from about 1890 to World War I. It was the era of the great magazines—*Harper's Monthly, Century, Scribner's, Cosmopolitan, Collier's Weekly*, and the rapidly-growing, five-cent *Saturday Evening Post*. They were called magazines because they were storehouses of miscellany—novels run serially, short stories, poems, cartoons, history, travel, science, invention, current events—but not so much emphasis on Great Problems as their successors. Generally there was more fiction than fact. Book publishers also turned out many more titles of fiction than of fact. Everything was illustrated, even the books of fiction, often with color pictures; it also became an age of fine printing.

The reading of novels was the great entertainment, and why not? There was no television, not even radio. Only in the latter half of the era were there silent movies, and the longest of them took scarcely a half-hour away from reading time. Everyone—except the types who now profess to despise television—was familiar with the six best sellers in fiction. Who wrote them might not be important—who remembers George Barr McCutcheon, Harold Magrath, Gene Stratton Porter, or even Harold Bell Wright? But everyone could identify Charles Dana Gibson of the Gibson girl, Harrison Fisher, James Montgomery Flagg. Who illustrated a book might be as important as who wrote it. Illustrators became specialists—military, historical, Western. Almost every Western illustrator at some time or other did Custer's Last Fight.

The two top Western illustrators, Frederic Remington and Charles M. Russell, contributed nothing distinctive to Custer Fight art. Their several works could as well have been used to illustrate almost anything else; and, in fact, many of them were. Both artists were in such demand that they tried to do pieces that would do double duty, triple duty, or whatever the traffic would bear.

Remington's pen-and-ink "Custer's Last Stand" that illustrated Major General James Grant Wilson's "Two Modern Knights Errant" in the July, 1891, *Cosmopolitan*, is credited "by courtesy of Mrs. Custer." Presumably Remington had given the original to her. It shows a few soldiers fighting a few Indians. Remington illustrated Godfrey's classic in the January, 1892, *Century*, but his "Indians Watching Custer's Advance" might have been watching anyone else's advance, or no advance at all. "Dismounted," "Boots and Saddles," and "Unhorsed" are equally generic.

Remington's painting "Custer's Last Charge," copyrighted 1895 for photogravure reproduction in *The Library of Historic Characters and Famous Events*, edited by A. R. Spofford, Frank Weitenkampf, and J. P. Lamberton, sticks closest to the subject—the leader of the horseman sabering dismounted Indians is recognizably Custer.[12] Remington's watercolor "Custer's Last Stand," a light wash sketch of possibly 1903, shows a half-dozen figures—one uniform coat is the only indication they might be soldiers—with others fading into the background, firing revolvers and rifles at mounted Indians. Two with almost identical features might be mistaken for Custer in a dim light or a poor reproduction. Remington's black-and-white oil "The Custer Fight on the Little Big Horn" must have had some exposure before it was used in the October, 1928, *Red Book Magazine* to illustrate Frazier Hunt's series that became *Custer, The Last of the Cavaliers*. It shows mounted Indians surrounding dim figures on a distant hill.

Other Remington pictures have been used as Little Big Horn illustrations, notably one originally called "The Last Stand." It was a product of Remington's tour as artist-correspondent for the Ghost Dance troubles, or Sioux War of 1890-91, and was used in a crude engraving signed Kurtz to illustrate added chapters on this war in the 1891 edition of *Wild Life on the Plains*. It appeared again in *Harper's Weekly*, January 10, 1893, with an explanatory note by Remington, describing it as "depicting the remnant of a body of United States troops . . . How many scenes of which this typical have been enacted on this continent, who can say?" This makes it clear enough that it was intended to be typical and not Custer. Remington used it as frontispiece for his *Pony Tracks*, 1895, containing his articles on the Sioux War of 1890-1891.[13] It was used again in 1907 in Randall Parrish's *The Great Plains*.[14] In all these appearances, the title is simply "The Last Stand," but somewhere along the line the original painting acquired a brass plate reading "Custer's Last Stand," and since 1939 it has been reproduced several times—six times at least—with that designation. To say it looks less like Custer's Last Stand than any of the other Remington works is indeed saying a lot.

A Remington oil called "Rounded Up" has some resemblances to a "last stand," but happily seems not to have been used as a Custer illustration. More curious are the uses of one that Frazier and Robert Hunt call "Indian Squaws Hurriedly Breaking Camp," in *I Fought with Custer: The Story of Sergeant Windolph*. They hedge a bit in saying that it "depicts what undoubtedly happened on the early afternoon of June 26, [sic.]

1876."[15] The same picture, but with the title "Indians Escaping after the Burning of Julesburg" is in Frank Gilbert Roe's *The Indian and the Horse*.[16] The same picture, but with the title "Death Cry of the Pawnees: Indian against Indian" appears in a publication by the editors of *Real West* magazine.[17]

Remington did some great Western paintings—but not about Custer.

Charles Marion Russell (1864-1926) painted his most notable "Custer's Last Stand" in 1903, **(plate XI)** and it was used that year to illustrate *Adventures with Indians and Game*, by Dr. William A. Allen.[18] It was also reproduced in a large-size stone lithograph. Prominent in its foreground is a large group of mounted Indians at full gallop; the "last stand" is so dim in the background as almost to fade out in some reproductions. Upon the assumption that there might be another, inquiry was made of H. F. Britzman, who at that time controlled a large number of unpublished Charlie Russell pictures that he was using to illustrate books under the imprint Trail's End Publishing Company, Pasadena, California. Mr. Britzman replied that he had indeed found a pen-and-ink drawing titled on the back "The Custer Fight" in Charlie Russell's handwriting. Unhappily it had been called "The Last of the Fetterman Command" in *Pen and Ink Drawings by Charles M. Russell, Book No. 2*, and also in *Forty Pen and Ink Drawings by Charles M. Russell* (combining Book No. 1 and Book No. 2) both published by Trail's End in 1947. The Fetterman fight label had been hung on it in *Back-Trailing on the Old Frontiers*, published in Great Falls, Montana, in 1922. The Fetterman fight took place in December, but the drawing shows a summer scene. This confirms Charlie's designation, but the picture has never been published with the title that he gave it.

If Britzman slipped on this one, he made up for it by correctly identifying another pen-and-ink drawing as "Curley the Crow Scout Brings News of the Custer Fight to the Steamer *Far West*." It was used with its proper title to illustrate *Firewater and Forked Tongues*, by M. I. McCreight, published by Trail's End in 1947. It had previously been used, just as a riverboat picture, to illustrate two books by Agnes C. Laut, *The Blazed Trail of the Old Frontier*, 1926, and *The Romance of the Rails*, 1929.[19]

Russell did some great Western pictures—but not about Custer.

Olaf Carl Seltzer (1877-1957) painted a very similar "Curley Bringing News of the Custer Massacre to the Steamer *Far West*." Seltzer, a Danish immigrant, came to Great Falls, Montana, the home of Charlie Russell in 1892. Russell was Seltzer's teacher, friend and, at times, rival; Seltzer for most of his life lived in Russell's shadow. Yet there are critics who acclaim O. C. Seltzer as one of the West's great artists. He was commissioned by

Plate XI. Charles M. Russell
Custer's Last Stand
Water color, 17 x 28½ inches, 1903
Courtesy of The Lovelace Foundation for Medical Education and Research, Albuquerque, New Mexico

Dr. Philip G. Cole to paint more than a hundred scenes relating to Montana history. For these Seltzer developed an unusual technique, for they were miniatures painted in oil, about 5 by 7 inches in size, sharp, clear, and detailed. They were done under magnification, and it is said that his eyes suffered, so that eventually he had to abandon this type of work. Seven of them relate to the Battle of the Little Big Horn. The titles are "Custer, Reno and Benteen with the Grey Horse Troop on the Eve of Custer's Massacre," "Trumpeter John Martin Bringing His Famous Last Message from Custer to Major Benteen," "Sitting Bull—Making Medicine," "Reno Routed," "Custer's Last Stand," the one about Curley, and "Lieut. Bradley's Discovery of Custer's Massacre." All are reproduced, some of them for the first time, in *Montana in Miniature*, published in 1966.[20] The Curley picture had been used in Colonel Graham's *The Custer Myth* with no indication of the artist's name,[21] and "Reno Routed" had had a couple of appearances.

Ernest L. Blumenschein (1874-1960) dated his Custer fight picture 1897. With the title "We Circled All Round Him," it was used in *McClure's Magazine* for September, 1898, to illustrate Hamlin Garland's "General Custer's Last Fight as Seen by Two Moon." It was that year, while on a sketching tour for *McClure's*, that Blumenschein first visited Taos, with which place and its artists' colony his name was to be prominently associated. His picture was used again as frontispiece for Cyrus Townsend Brady's *Indian Fights and Fighters* in 1904, with the title changed to "The Last of Custer." Before Blumenschein got going on the New Mexico landscapes for which he is famed, he returned to Custer subject matter once more in illustrating Randall Parrish's *Molly McDonald*, a tale of Custer's Washita campaign.

Joseph Henry Sharp (1859-1953) called the father of the Taos colony, painted a landscape "The Custer Battlefield," in 1908. William Herbert Dunton (1878-1936), also associated with Taos, did a "Custer's Last Stand," **(plate XII)** reproduced in 1915.[22]

There were others who made their mark in the era of the great illustrators. Rufus Fairchild Zogbaum (1848-1925) specialized in military subjects. Much of his best work is assembled in his *Horse, Foot, and Dragoons*, 1888. His work is to be found in Elizabeth B. Custer's *Following the Guidon*, and in General Charles King's *A War-time Wooing*, and *The Iron Brigade*. His battle pieces include "The First Minnesota Regiment at the Battle of Gettysburg" and others from Lake Erie to Manila Bay. His "Arrival of Terry's Column on the Custer Battlefield" illustrated General

Plate XII. William Herbert Dunton
The Custer Fight
Oil on canvas, 32 x 50 inches, date unknown
The Whitney Gallery of Western Art, Cody, Wyoming

George A. Forsyth's *The Story of the Soldier*, 1900. Zogbaum's "The Last Stand," however, is not about Custer; it originally illustrated General Wesley Merritt's account of the Ute campaign of 1879 in *Harper's Magazine* for April, 1890.

Charles Schreyvogel (1861-1912) was acclaimed for "My Bunkie," 1899. This, and his "The Skirmish Line," 1900, and "The Circle Attack" have been used to illustrate the Little Big Horn, but it seems doubtful if they were so intended. His outstanding Custer picture "Custer's Demand," 1903 related to the 1868-69 campaign. J. Steeple Davis, painter of battle scenes, illustrated King's *The General's Double*, and the like. His "Custer's Last Fight," 1897, is a spirited one, handsomely engraved in "The Edition De Luxe" of *The History of Our Country*, by Edward S. Ellis, frontispiece of the 1910 printing. *Ellis's History of the United States*, 1899, Volume IV has the same picture, poorly engraved and worse-printed. A sepia ink improved it in some other edition of this hardy perennial, and it is also to be found in Smith Burnham's *The Making of Our Country*, 1921.

A prowl through these multivolume subscription-book histories of the long-forgotten Age of Self-Improvement turns up another "Custer's Last Stand and Death" that had considerable exposure. In early versions it is credited "Copyright O. Reich, 1888;" later on, the artist's name is lost to fame. The earliest found was in Volume III, page 288 of *Six Thousand Years of History* in ten volumes by Edgar Sanderson, A.M., J. P. Lamberton, A.M., John McGovern and several more, 1899, copyright 1899. It shows up again in a 1900 printing of *The World's History and Its Makers*, by the same authors, but a different publisher, and the picture still on page 288 of Volume III. About all we can add on O. Reich is that he did "The Battle of Bunker Hill," also copyright 1888, in the same volume. Now turning to the *Library of Universal History* in 12 volumes, compiled, arranged and written by Israel Smith Clare with an introduction by Moses Coit Tyler, we find Reich's Custer on page 2921 of Volume IX of the 1900 printing, with an 1898 copyright. A year later, 1901, the same publishers brought out *Sixty Centuries of Human Progress*, by the same authors, also 12 volumes, with O. Reich still in Volume IX, but upped ten pages to 2931—and this time the copyright date is 1889, which is close to the time Reich produced his picture. This is not all. *The Great Republic by the Master Historians*, edited by Charles Morris and Oliver H. G. Leigh gets around to Custer in its Volume III in 1901 and 1902 printings, copyright 1897, and, enrolling bigger names, *The History of the United States*, by James Wilford Garner and Henry Cabot Lodge, with a historical review by John Bach McMaster is dated 1905, with the Reich Custer in its Volume

IV. Reich rides on into 1923 with *The Wonder Book of Knowledge,* compiled and edited by Henry Chase Hill.

Edwin Willard Deming (1860-1942) had many associations with Remington. They shared the illustration of two of King's novels, *A Daughter of the Sioux* and *An Apache Princess.* Both saw something of the Sioux War of 1890-1891. Deming is remembered for his Indian illustrations, including a long series of juveniles with his wife Therese. His "The Grand Charge That Ended the Fight," sometimes called "Custer's Last Stand" **(plate XIII)** illustrated one of Brady's articles that became *Indian Fights and Fighters.* A. Berghaus, who shared with Remington the illustrating of Mrs. Custer's Tenting on the Plains did a Custer fight for a dime-novel color cover, *Custer's Last Shot; or, The Boy Trailer of the Little Big Horn,* by Colonel J. M. Travers, pseudonym for St. George Rathborne, published in Frank Tousey's *Pluck and Luck* No. 235. R. Farrington Elwell (1874-1962) was a protege of William F. Cody, and his early work includes posters for Buffalo Bill's Wild West and illustrations for Cody's *True Tales of the Plains.* He worked as illustrator for books and magazines, but his Custer subjects were latter-day paintings not used as illustration. They are "Custer's Last Stand," "Custer's Last March," and "Victory Smoke."

The illustrator almost everyone remembers is Newell Convers Wyeth (1882-1945). He was doing Western subjects as early as 1903—a *Saturday Evening Post* cover for an Emerson Hough story. He illustrated Frank H. Spearman's *Whispering Smith,* novels by Alfred Henry Lewis, Stewart Edward White, Randall Parrish, and Clarence E. Mulford, and Buffalo Bill's last autobiography. N. C. Wyeth's "Custer's Last Stand" was used in 1932 in an advertising series, "Nature in the Raw is Seldom Mild," to point up that Lucky Strike cigarettes were "toasted." That was in the lean years of illustrating. About the period of World War I, publishers discovered that readers wanted to imagine what the hero and heroine looked like, without being influenced by the ideas of Wyeth, Pyle, Yohn and their like. The fact was that it was becoming too expensive to tip in by hand each separately printed picture at the exact page where it matched the text. So the illustrating of fiction was abandoned. It was a decade or so before publishers discovered that a book's dust wrapper could be something more than a piece of wrapping paper to keep dust off a book until it was sold. Thereafter books were illustrated and advertised with jacket designs. When paperback publishers took up the idea for their covers, there was complaint that some books were being underillustrated and overadvertised—some of them could drag a sex motif out of a most unpromising reprint title. Wyeth survived. In the lean years he illustrated

48

Plate XIII. Edwin W. Deming
Custer's Last Stand
Oil on Canvas, 34x60 inches, date unknown
Courtesy of Miss Alden Deming, New York, New York

classics for the Christmas gift-book trade, and when dust wrappers went to four-color he returned to fiction illustrating.[23]

There were artists who did no illustrating, but most of those called Western artists got around to Custer some time or other. One of the least likely to have done a "Battle of the Little Big Horn" was John Adams Elder (1833-1895) of Fredericksburg, Virginia. Elder was born in Fredericksburg and died in Fredericksburg; it was only after a shell fired in the Battle of Fredericksburg set his bed afire that Elder left home and joined the Confederate army. However he had studied under Emanuel Leutze, painter of "Washington Crossing the Delaware," not only in Fredericksburg, but also in Dusseldorf, Germany. This accounts for Elder's interest in battle pictures. He added personal experience in his "The Battle of the Crater," and other Civil War subjects. Elder also did genre pictures of scenes familiar to him in the South, and many portraits, most of them of Confederate generals and political figures, including Lee and Jefferson Davis. In 1884, the era of Heroes of the Plains and Buffalo Bill's Wild West, Elder added the Custer fight to his battle pieces. Elder is considered a realist of the Eakins tradition and his "Battle of the Little Big Horn" **(plate XIV)** has had critical approval.[24]

William Robinson Leigh (1866-1955) devoted most of his long lifetime to Western subjects and won wide recognition as an artist. Although reproductions of his works are in many books, he was not primarily an illustrator. His "Custer's Last Fight" has the familiar pattern of mounted Indians in foreground; Custer and troopers dimly outlined in background, but Leigh rounds out this obvious idea with plenty of action (and some lack of technical accuracy). An early book use was in Fairfax Downey's *Indian-Fighting Army,* 1941. Subsequently Leigh's painting was reproduced on two book jackets and as a paperback cover.[25]

Thomas Hart Benton, born in Neosho, Missouri, in 1889, painted "Custer's Last Stand—Inspired by the St. Louis Bar Room Picture"[26] in 1945 as modernization of a subject by then recognized as folk art. Even if he had not said so, you would know he had the Anheuser-Busch lithograph in mind, for it shows up to the right of the bar in his mural of the ballad of "Frankie and Johnnie." While it cannot be said that Benton did not treat the subject seriously, the sense of tragedy is lacking.

Walt Kuhn (1877-1949) took a step further from reality to mythology in his series called "An Imaginary History of the West." His "Wild West #1" 1919 **(frontispiece),** and "Wild West #2"[27] give a humorous twist to the Custer fight. Many cartoonists have handled it less than seriously,

Plate XIV. John Elder
Battle of the Little Big Horn
Oil on canvas, 54⅝x84⅛ inches, 1885
Permanent loan to Amon Carter Museum, courtesy of The State of New York, Division of Military and Naval Affairs

notably Stan Lynde (born in Billings, Montana, in 1931) in his cartoon-strip parody of the Western, "Rick O'Shay."[28]

In comic books, so called, the cartoonists play it straight. Decorators of maps often use caricature when they play it straight or may intentionally imitate some recognizable composition. When W. Langdon Kihn is employed by *National Geographic Magazine* to illustrate an extended record series on Indians of the Americas it is to be expected that he will get around to the Custer fight. Books of similar character may demand a Custer fight picture as in Lorence F. Bjorklund's illustrations for *Indian Wars and Warriors West* by Paul Wellman. Little Big Horn depictors have not lacked opportunity in jacket designs, paperback covers, newspaper and magazine features, sensational discoveries for the pulp Westerns, and the perennial illustrated juveniles. James Daugherty (born in 1889 in Asheville, North Carolina), a Newbery Medal winner, has done a number of Custer pictures for juveniles. A paperback cover by Frank McCarthy for Ernest Haycox's *Bugles in the Afternoon* won the recognition of the Society of Illustrators in 1963.

What is less to be expected is continuing production of Custer fight pictures for no particular illustrative purpose. Harold Von Schmidt's "There Was a Man: Custer's Last Stand" was reproduced in full color in a foldout for the September, 1950, issue of *Esquire*, a magazine that went in more for girls than gore, yet it was "painted expressly" for that publication with a brief article by Stewart H. Holbrook obviously tailored to the picture. William Reusswig's "Custer's Last Stand" was reproduced in color in similar fashion for the June 30, 1951, issue of *Collier's*. Dwight Franklin applied the arts of sculpture to the Custer fight. Walter S. Oschman's "Custer at the Battle of the Little Big Horn" missed use as a calendar picture, but was twice reproduced in color by the *Chicago Tribune*, once in the Sunday magazine, and once on page one, with an anniversary article.

The enthusiasms that result in the private printing of pamphlets by E. E. McVey, *(The Crow Scout Who Killed Custer*, illustrated by Stanley Legowick) and Ken Lizorty *(June 25, 1876, Custer's Last Stand)* are explicable. But only a continuing public interest can account for an artist of the stature of James Kenneth Ralston (born 1896 on a ranch near Choteau, Montana) virtually devoting a career to painting every aspect of the Little Big Horn fight. A count of 17, which may not be comprehensive, includes oil paintings, a mural, and pen-and-ink sketches. He is also author of a separately published poem, *The Custer Mystery*. The 18-foot-long "After the Battle," 1955, showing Indians plundering the bodies after

52

Plate XV. J. Smith
Untitled
Oil on canvas, 25½x54 inches, date unknown
Courtesy of Mr. A. Fristoe Nelson, Seattle, Washington

the last stand, is said to depict "thirty-nine known incidents relating to the Custer fight." It was shown on the Montana Centennial Train and at the New York World's Fair of 1964. Other oils include "Custer's Last Hope," 1959, "Prelude to Tragedy," "His Last Salute," "Muggins Taylor Leaves Fort Pease with the Custer Massacre Message," and the painting at Custer Battlefield, "Call of the Bugle: Custer Gathers the Survivors for the Last Stand," 1965. Ralston has, however, done a few non-Custer paintings: "A Bronc in the Breaks," "A Steer Outfit," 1960, "Return of a War Party," "Leader of the Fur Brigade," and "The Crossing, 1864," for the Montana Historical Society in 1965.[29]

Paralleling the continuing interest in Custer as subject for painter, poet, and cartoonist, for folklore and folk art, legend, literature, and sub-literature was a growing serious study of the fight by historians, professional, amateur, and enthusiast, and as corollary, a demand for accuracy in its pictorial representation.

Major Edward Smith Luce wrote his *Keogh, Comanche and Custer* (1939) before going to Custer Battlefield where, during a long superintendency, he devoted himself to study of the fight, introducing the use of metal-detectors to trace routes and lines of battle. His choice for pictorial accuracy was "General Custer's letzte schlacht," which translates "last fight," painted by Elk Eber (1892-1944) for the Karl May Museum, Radebaul bei Dresden, Germany. Major Luce pointed to a Custer with close-cropped hair, firing a pistol (no saber), "the soldier who talked with his bugle," mentioned by the Indian woman Little Shield; the soldier having trouble with the breech of his carbine; Indians with bows and arrows as well as Winchester rifles. (There was a slip in showing a regimental standard.) The story told was that Elk Eber's mother was a Sioux named Little Elk, who had quit Buffalo Bill's Wild West while it was touring Germany in 1889 and had married a professor; and that the picture was based on her recollections of the Custer fight as told to her son.

Publication of this story brought a rebuttal from Hermann Eber, son of the painter, who sent a copy of a birth certificate showing that his father Wilhelm Emil Eber was born in Haardt, April 18, 1892, the son of Friedrich Wilhelm Eber, a wine dealer, and Rosa Sibylla née Eisele, who of course was no Indian. It was admitted that the painter changed his name from Emil to Elk, and did not deny the story, which perhaps originated in some publicity-writer's imagination. This is not incongruous in a museum commemorating a great fiction writer, Karl May (1842-1912) whose juvenile adventure stories were immensely popular in Europe, especially those featuring a Western scout, Old Shatterhand, and an Indian hero, Winnetou. They were translated into many languages, including English, but such incongruities as ostrich hunts on the plains of Nebraska caused American publishers to shy away from them. The museum owed much to Patty Frank, a veteran of Buffalo Bill's Wild West as the cowboy Isto Maza, whose real name was Ernst Tobis. Despite his own fondness for exotic aliases, Patty Frank is said to have doubted Elk Eber's romantic story. Eber's picture, however, was reproduced in National Parks Service handbooks of Custer Battlefield and in a number of books.[30]

The Karl May Museum boasts two other Custer pictures, both painted by Carl Lindeberg, "Beginning of the Charge that Wiped Out Custer," and "Das Ende" (the end; finding the bodies).

When Colonel Graham compiled his collection of Custer source material as *The Custer Myth,* he and his publishers sought an accurate fight picture. The artist was Gayle Porter Hoskins, long a resident of Wilmington, Delaware; it is known that he had been born in Brazil, Indiana, in 1887, that he had been a student of the Art Institute of Chicago and of Howard Pyle, but no record of the date of his death has been found. Hoskins painted scenes of both world wars and historical subjects featuring firearms. His "The Battle of the Little Big Horn," 1928,[31] had been used in a 1930 calendar by Brown & Bigelow. For his "Custer's Last Fight," 1953, he used a clay model of the battlefield, based on a United States Geological Survey contoured map, on which Colonel Graham indicated troop movements. The painting was reproduced in color on both jacket and endpapers of the book, with key, and also as a separate color print.

A similar problem was faced by John E. Parsons and John S. duMont for their brochure, *Firearms in the Custer Battle.* The artist chosen was Theodore B. Pitman (1892-1956). Pitman was a graduate of Harvard, a captain of field artillery in World War I, colonel in the OSS in World War II, business man, gun collector, polo player, and by avocation a maker of museum dioramas, including one of the Battle of Bunker Hill. His first "Custer's Last Stand," 1923, **(plate XVI)** was "painted expressly for" Colonel Homer W. Wheeler's *The Frontier Trail,* reissued as *Buffalo Days.* In Pitman's second "Custer's Last Stand," 1953, John duMont points out, Custer is correctly shown with English "Bulldog" revolvers, wearing the blue shirt mentioned in the Reno court of inquiry testimony, and with hair cut short. Some Indians are wearing items that Colonel Pitman obtained from participants in the fight.[32]

James S. Hutchins, whose interests are indicated in an article "The Cavalry Campaign Outfit at the Little Big Horn," which he wrote for the *Military Collector & Historian,* has a passion for accuracy regarding

Plate XVI. Theodore B. Pitman
Custer's Last Stand
Oil on canvas, 24 x 36¼ inches, 1923
Courtesy of Mrs. S. A. Rockwell, Cambridge, Massachusetts

such items as saddles, saddlebags, cartridge boxes, and such gear. In 1956 he commissioned Nick Eggenhofer to paint "To the Last Man, June 25, 1876." It was reproduced in color in *The Westerners New York Posse Brand Book*, Volume IV, Number 1, 1957, and issued also as a separate print. Nick Eggenhofer was born in 1897 in Gauting, near Munich, Bavaria. He came to New Jersey in 1913, worked for a lithograph company in New York, and studied at Cooper Union. He wrote and illustrated *Wagons, Mules and Men* in 1961, and illustrated Western books by Ramon F. Adams, Wayne Gard, David Lavender, Mari Sandoz, and many others. His other Custer fight pictures include illustrations for Margaret Leighton's *The Story of General Custer*.

H. Charles McBarron is called "the dean of American military artists" by the Office, Chief of Military History, Headquarters, Department of the Army, which published a series of twenty paintings under the heading *The American Soldier*, representing various historic periods. McBarron also contributed to the battle series, *The Army in Action*. His "Custer's Last Stand" was one of a series of eight Americana subjects done for the American Oil Company in 1962. We can be sure that the 7th Cavalry troopers represented here are authentic.

Now, all this is not to insinuate that, for authenticity concerning that storied terrain, one is obliged to consult only Hoskins; that for correctness in the firearms one can trust only Pitman; that for exactness in the uniforms one must believe only McBarron; or that one can depend only upon Eggenhofer for genuineness in the equipment. It is, however, worth pointing out that, in spite of the progressive perfecting of one or another of the numberless details of this event that has so fascinated so many for so long—or perhaps because of that very same process—there seems no end to the continuing demand that the pictorial record of the Custer fight be redone again and again until it is set aright.

This compulsion hardly touches other facets of American history. Leutze's "Washington Crossing the Delaware" has been derided for a century and longer; yet it is tolerated, and the subject is rarely redepicted. But Custer must be rid of the figmentary sabers, the invented flags, and the imagined dress uniforms wished upon him by lithographers and wood-cut carvers as we strive to authenticate the record of this perennial legend.

Still, the haunting question will remain when the correct English "Bulldog" revolvers, the swallow-tailed guidons with stars of gilt, and the blue shirts and saddlebags are all finally painted in: who, among the hundreds of artists, has shown The Last Stand exactly as it really happened?

NOTES

1. J. M. Carnahan to E. A. Brininstool, Mar. 13, 1925, in Brininstool collection.

2. James Taylor Forrest, "What a sight it was!" in *American Heritage*, February, 1961, Vol. XII, No. 2, pp. 46-55.

3. Library of Congress, *An Album of American Battle Art*, Washington, 1947, pp. 165-67; *American Heritage*, August, 1963, Vol. XIV, No. 5, pp. 2, 54-61; December, 1963, Vol. XV, No. 1, pp. 30-31, 106-107.

4. I have uncolored lithographs of the battles of Fort Henry and Memphis, purchased by a sailor on leave after he had taken part in these battles and framed by him in 1863 (he used newspapers dated July, 1863, as backing). He was killed before the was was over, leaving these memorials of his service to his family.

5. Colin Simkin, editor, *Currier and Ives' America*, Crown Publishers, Inc., New York, 1952; Carl W. Drepperd, *Early American Prints*, Century Co., New York, London 1930.

6. Judson Elliott Walker, *Campaigns of General Custer in the North-West, and the Final Surrender of Sitting Bull*, New York, 1881, reprinted for University Microfilms, Inc., Ann Arbor, by Argonaut Press, Ltd., New York, 1966, pp. 114-20, mentions Mulvany working on an engraving and reprints Walt Whitman's appreciation; Robert Taft, "The Pictorial Record of the Old West," in *Kansas Historical Quarterly*, November, 1946, Vol. XIV, No. 4, pp. 368-77, with reproduction from the original painting.

7. Cassilly Adams, Declaration for Invalid Pension, filed Apr. 29, 1906, with amendments June 14, 1906, March 11, 1907, and May 25, 1912. This and a vast file of information about Cassilly Adams comes from Lina Adams (Mrs. C. Cassilly Adams, widow of the son of the artist), including family history, letters from William Apthorp Adams, another son of the artist, and other members of the family, reports from the National Archives and copyright office, and much more resulting from her research. Much of the original material and a collection of sketches and paintings by Cassilly Adams she donated in 1963 to the Buffalo Bill Historical Center, Cody, Wyoming.

8. Don Russell, "Sixty Years in Bar Rooms; or, *Custer's Last Fight*," in *The Westerners Brand Book*, Chicago, November, 1946, Vol. III, No. 9, with much added data; Edward S. Luce to Don Russell, June 20, 1946.

9. Anheuser-Busch, Inc., *"Custer's Last Battle,"* a 10-page pamphlet sent with the lithographs; George W. Eads of Anheuser-Busch, Inc., to Don Russell, June 28, 1946, quoting letter from F. Otto Becker; Roland F. Becker to Don Russell, Dec. 18, 1947.

10. K. Ross Toole, "E. S. Paxson, Neglected Artist of the West," and Michael Kennedy, "Frontier Vermeer," in *Montana*, Spring, 1954, Vol. IV, No. 2, pp. 24-41; Franz R. Stenzel, "E. S. Paxson, Montana Artist," in *Montana*, Autumn, 1963, Vol. XIII, No. 4, pp. 50-76; W. E. Paxson, *"Custer's Last Stand*, The Painting and the Artist," in *True West*, October, 1963, Vol. XI, No. 2, pp. 14-16, 52-53; William Edgar Paxson to Don Russell, Feb. 28, 1965; printed information sheets from Paxson Gallery of Western Art, including "About the Artist," and the artist's description of the Custer picture.

11. Wilbur G. Kurtz, *The Atlanta Cyclorama*, City of Atlanta, 1954, pp. 24-28; Milwaukee Art Center, *An Exhibition in Tribute to Richard Lorenz*, Milwaukee, 1966.

12. William Finley & Co., Philadelphia, 1895, Vol. X, p. 252.

13. Harper & Brothers, New York, 1895; reprints by Long's College Book Co., Columbus, Ohio, 1951; University of Oklahoma Press, Norman, 1961.

14. A. C. McClurg & Co., Chicago, 1907, p. 228.

15. Charles Scribner's Sons, New York, London, 1947, p. 43.

16. University of Oklahoma Press, Norman, 1955, pp. 206-207.

17. *Wars of the American Indian*, Americana Library Book No. 3, Winter, 1964, pp. 38-39.

18. A. W. Bowen & Co., Chicago, 1903, p. 64.

19. Both by Robert M. McBride and Company, New York, *Blazed Trail*, p. 245, as "The First Trip of the Season;" *Romance of the Rails*, Vol. I, p. 7.

20. Edited by Van Kirke Nelson and Cato K. Butler,

with the notes on the pictures by Dr. Cole, printed in Kalispell, Montana.

21. *The Custer Myth*, p. 7.

22. Jeff C. Dykes, "Tentative Bibliographic Check Lists of Western Illustrators" in *The American Book Collector*, beginning in April, 1963, (Vol. XIII, No. 8, includes Blumenschein, Deming, Dunton, Elwell, and some others. For the Taos group, Van Deren Coke, *Taos and Santa Fe: The Artist's Environment*, University of New Mexico Press, 1963; P. T. Farnsworth, "Folk-Lore of a Vanishing Race Preserved in the Paintings of Edwin Willard Deming," *The Craftsman*, May, 1906, Vol. X, No. 2.

23. Helen L. Card, *Catalog No. Five*, New York, n.d. has a checklist of N. C. Wyeth.

24. Virginia Museum of Fine Arts, *A Retrospective Exhibition* of the Work of John Adams Elder, Richmond, 1947.

25. W. R. Leigh, "My America" in *Arizona Highways*, February, 1948; "Sagebrush Rembrandt," in *Collier's*, Nov. 11, 1950; *Time*.

26. Benton's title in a 1966 note to Don Russell; in a 1946 catalogue of Associated American Artists Galleries, Chicago, the subtitle is "Bar Room Picture in the St. Louis Mode," and I go along with Benton on the change. For "Frankie and Johnnie," see Ernest A. Irvine, *The Benton

Murals in the Missouri State Capitol*, Vandalia Leader, 1939, and post card reproductions by Tolson Drug Co., Jefferson City.

27. Fred S. Bartlett, *Walt Kuhn, An Imaginary History of the West*, Amon Carter Museum of Western Art and Colorado Springs Fine Arts Center, 1964.

28. *Chicago Tribune, Billings Gazette,* and other newspapers, Oct. 14, 1965; for data on Lynde, *The Westerners Brand Book*, Chicago, July, 1964, Vol. XXI, No. 5, p. 38.

29. Michael Kennedy, "Man-Who-Avoids-the-Footprints-of-C.M.R." in *Montana*, Spring, 1961, Vol. XI, No. 2, pp. 25-43.

30. Don Russell, "Sixty Years in Bar Rooms," *The Westerners Brand Book*, November, 1946; "More on Custer Art," July, 1948; Dr. Rudolf Beissel, "The Karl May Museum," June, 1961.

31. Title used by artist, Gayle P. Hoskins to Don Russell, Mar. 25, 1949; this picture also has been commended for accuracy.

32. John S. duMont to Don Russell, Feb. 3, 1953; John S. duMont, "Theodore Baldwin Pitman—A Tribute," in *The Westerners New York Posse Brand Book*, Vol. IV, No. 1, pp. 11-12, 23.

BIBLIOGRAPHY

A comprehensive bibliography of Custer, or of the Battle of the Little Big Horn, would probably require more pages than there are in this book. Listed here are some of the important Custer items; a considerable number more, some of them quite unimportant, that gain entry because of their illustrations; and a few more or less obscure items about the artists. Names in parenthesis are those of illustrators. Pictures separately published (lithographs, for example) are not listed.

Adams, Jacob, *A Story of the Custer Massacre*, Robert G. Hayman reprint, Carey, Ohio, 1965

Alascia, Nicholas, *Billy the Kid*, July 1966, Charlton Comics

Album of American Battle Art, Library of Congress, Washington, 1947

Alexander, Hartley B., *Sioux Indian Paintings*, C. Szwedzicki, Nice, France, 1938 (Amos Bad Heart Bull : Kills Two)

Allen, William A., *Adventures with Indians and Game*, A. W. Bowen & Co., Chicago, 1903 (C. A. Russell)

Amaral, Anthony A., *Comanche*, Westernlore, Los Angeles, 1961

Anheuser-Busch, Inc., *"Custer's Last Battle,"* St. Louis, n.d.

Appel, David, *Comanche*, World, Cleveland, New York, 1951 (Daugherty)

Armour, Richard, *It All Started with Columbus*, Bantam, 1965 (Campbell Grant)

Avon Periodicals, Inc., *Custer's Last Fight*, New York, 1950

Barker, Eugene C., Dodd, William E., Webb, Walter P., *Our Nation Grows Up*, Row, Peterson & Co., Evanston, Illinois, 1938 (Dorothy Todd)

Barnes, Charles, and Hawker, Marshall, *New National Fifth Reader*, A. S. Barnes & Co., New York, Cincinnati, Chicago, 1884 (W. M. Cary)

Bartlett, Fred S., *Walt Kuhn, An Imaginary History of the West*, Amon Carter Museum of Western Art and Colorado Springs Fine Art Center, 1964

Bates, Charles Francis, *Custer's Indian Battles*, Bronxville, New York, 1936

———, *Westchester-Hudson River-West Point*, Robert Bruce, New York n.d. (J. W. Evans)

Beardsley, J. L., "Custer's Troop of Doom," *Big-Book Western*, December-January, 1937-38

Beisel, Rudolf, "The Karl May Museum," *The Westerners Brand Book*, Chicago, June, 1961

Beitz, Les, "Will Crawford, Wizard of Pen and Ink," *True West*, September-October, 1967

Beyer, W. F. and Keydal, O. F., *Deeds of Valor*, Perrien-Keydal Co., Detroit, 1907 (C. D. Graves, Geo. Henderson)

Bonte, George Willard, *America Marches Past*, D. Appleton-Century, New York, 1936

Bordeaux, William J., *Custer's Conqueror* (C. A. Schmitt)

Bradley, James H., *The March of the Montana Column*, edited by Edgar I. Stewart, University of Oklahoma Press, Norman, 1961

Brady, Cyrus Townsend, *Britton of the Seventh*, A. C. McClurg & Co., Chicago, 1914 (The Kinneys)

———, *Indian Fights and Fighters*, Doubleday, Page & Co., Garden City, New York, 1909 (Blumenschein)

———, "War with the Sioux, Part II," *Pearson's*, September, 1904 (E. W. Deming)

Breihan, Carl W., "Last Word on Custer's Last Stand," *Outdoor Adventures* July, 1956 (Maurice Bower)

Brininstool, E. A., *A Trooper with Custer*, Hunter-Trader-Trapper Co., Columbus, O., 1925

———, *Troopers with Custer*, Stackpole, Harrisburg, 1952 (Joe Wolf)

Brishan, Carl, "Who Was the Woman with Custer?" *Real West*, November, 1958

Brooks, Elbridge S., *The Master of the Strong Hearts*, E. P. Dutton & Co., New York, 1898 (W. M. Cary)

Buel, J. W., *Heroes of the Plains*, Cincinnati Publishing Co., 1884 (Armand Welcker)

Buffalo Bill and His Wild West Companions, Henneberry Co., Chicago, n.d. (J. Manz & Co., engravers)

Buffalo Bill's Wild West, Programme Officiel, Paris, 1905

Bureau of Indian Affairs, *Famous Indians*, Washington, 1966 (Kicking Bear)

Caswell, Peter, "The Bar Room Custer," *Military Affairs*, Spring, 1947

Catalogue Thomas Hart Benton Paintings, Associated American Artists Galleries, Chicago, 1946

Chandler, Melbourne C., *Of GarryOwen in Glory*, Seventh United States Cavalry Association, 1961

Cheney, Louise, "Lounsberry's Famous News Scoop," *Real West*, September, 1964 (Robert Gleason)

Chrisman, Harry E., "George Phippen, Western Artist," *The West*, November, 1966

Clare, Israel Smith, editor, *Library of Universal History*, Union Book Co., New York, Chicago, 1900, IX (O. Reich)
_____,*Sixty Centuries of Human Progress*, Union Book Co., New York, 1901, IX (O. Reich)

Clarke, Donald Henderson, as told to, *The Autobiography of Frank Tarbeaux*, Vanguard, New York, 1930

Cody, William F., *Story of the Wild West and Camp-Fire Chats*, Historical Publishing Co., Philadelphia, 1888

Coffeen, Herbert, *The Custer Battle Book*, Carleton Press, New York, 1964, reprint of *The Teepee Book*, Sheridan, Wyoming, 1916, 1926

Coke, Van Deren, *Taos and Santa Fe: The Artist's Environment*, University of New Mexico Press, Albuquerque, 1963

Cole, Philip G., *Montana in Miniature*, edited by Van Kirke Nelson, Kalispell, Montana, 1966 (Olaf C. Seltzer)

Crawford, Captain Jack, *The Poet Scout*, H. Keller & Co., San Francisco, 1879; Funk & Wagnalls, New York, 1888

Crichton, Robert, with Miller, David, "Custer's Last Stand: Legend—or Blunder?," *Argosy*, May 1956 (Walter Baumhofer)

Curry, Tom, and Cowan, Wood, *Famous Figures of the Old West*, Monarch Books, Inc., Derby, Connecticut, 1965 Wood Cowan)

Custer, Elizabeth B., *Boots and Saddles*, Harper, New York, 1885; University of Oklahoma Press, Norman, 1961
_____,*Following the Guidon*, Harper, New York, 1890; University of Oklahoma Press, Norman, 1966
_____,*Tenting on the Plains*, Charles L. Webster & Co., New York, 1887; Harper, New York, 1895

Custer, General George A., *My Life on the Plains*, Sheldon & Co., New York, 1874; University of Oklahoma Press, Norman, 1962; University of Nebraska Press, Lincoln, 1966; reprinted with added material and pictures, as *Wild Life on the Plains*, Sun Publishing Co., St. Louis, 1883; Royal Publishing Co., St. Louis, 1891 (Barnsley, Remington)
_____,"War Memoirs," *Galaxy*, July-October, 1876

Cyclorama of Custer's Last Fight, Boston Cyclorama Co., 1889

Dallas, David, *Comanche Lives Again*, Centennial Publishing Co., Manhattan, Kansas, 1954

Dellenbaugh, Frederick S., *George Armstrong Custer*, Macmillan, New York, 1917

DeWolff, J. H., *Pawnee Bill*, Pawnee Bill's Historic Wild West Co., 1902

Downey, Fairfax, *Indian-Fighting Army*, Scribner's, New York, 1941 (W. R. Leigh)

Dugard, W. T., "The True Story of Custer's Last Stand," as told to Frank Smith, *Frontier Stories*, Fall, 1938 (Karl Mayor)

duMont, John S., "Theodore Baldwin Pitman—A Tribute," *The Westerners New York Posse Brand Book*, IV, no. 1.

Dustin, Fred, *The Custer Tragedy*, Edwards Bros., Ann Arbor, Michigan, 1939, reprint, 1965
_____,*Echoes from the Little Big Horn Fight*, Saginaw, Michigan, 1953

Dykes, Jeff C., "Tentative Bibliographic Check Lists of Western Illustrators," *American Book Collector*, beginning April, 1963

Echohawk, Brummett, "The Best Horse I Ever Rode," *Western Horseman*, January, 1956; "The Spotted Horse Alone," August, 1964

Eggleston, Edward, *The New Century History of the United States*, American Book Co., 1907 (L. Bettz)

Ellis, Edward S., *Ellis' History of the United States*, Holman-Taylor, Cleveland, 1899, IV (J. Steeple Davis)
_____,*The History of Our Country*, Jones Bros., Cincinnati, 1910, VI (J. Steeple Davis)
_____,*Indian Wars of the United States*, Cassell, New York, 1892, (A. R. Waud)
_____,and Charles F. Horne, *The Story of the Greatest Nations*, Auxiliary Educational League, New York, 1921, IX, (W. M. Cary)

Farnsworth, P. T., "Folk-Lore of a Vanishing Race Preserved in the Paintings of Edwin Willard Deming," *The Craftsman*, May, 1906, X, no. 2.

Finerty, John F., *War-Path and Bivouac*, Donohue & Henneberry, Chicago, 1890; University of Oklahoma Press, Norman, 1961 (John Mulvany)

Fletcher, Robert H., *Free Grass to Fences*, University Publishers, Inc., New York, 1960 (H. von Schmidt)

Fletcher, Sydney E., *The Big Book of the Wild West*, Grosset & Dunlap, New York, 1952

Foote, Irving H., *The Story of Our Republic*, State of Kansas, 1934, (Leon D'Emo, E. D. Weldon)

Forman, John Frederick, "Custer's Greatest Blunder," *Real West*, September, 1965 (Earl Norem)

Forrest, James Taylor, "What a Sight It Was!" (about W. M. Cary) *American Heritage*, February, 1961

Forsyth, Brevet Brig. Gen. George A., *The Story of the Soldier*, D. Appleton & Co., New York, 1900 (R. F. Zogbaum)

Fougera, Katherine Gibson, *With Custer's Cavalry*, Caxton Printers, Caldwell, Idaho, 1940

Fox, Norman, "Only the Dead Ride Proudly," *Blue Book*, June, 1948, (John McDermott)

Frost, Lawrence A., *The Custer Album*, Superior, Seattle, 1964

Gall, Alice, and Crew, Fleming, *Each in His Way*, Oxford University Press, London, New York, Toronto, 1937 (Kurt Wiese)

Gardner, Albert Ten Eyck, introduction, *101 Masterpieces of American Primitive Painting from the Collection of Edgar William & Bernice Chrysler Garbisch*, American Federation of Arts, 1961, (W. J. Wallack)

Garland, Hamlin, "General Custer's Last Fight as Seen by Two Moon," *McClure's*, September, 1898, XI, no. 5 (E. L. Blumenschein)

Garner, James Wilford, and Lodge, Henry Cabot, *The History of the United States*, Howard-Severance, Chicago, 1906 IV (O. Reich)

Garst, Shannon, *Crazy Horse, Great Warrior of the Sioux*, Houghton Mifflin, Boston, 1950 (William Moyers)

_____, *Custer, Fighter of the Plains*, Messner, New York, 1944 (Harve Stein)

_____, *Sitting Bull, Champion of His People*, Messner, New York, 1946 (E. C. Fax)

Godfrey, E. S., "Custer's Last Battle," *Century*, January, 1892, (Remington; numerous reprints, some with illustrations)

_____, *The Field Diary of Lt. Edward Settle Godfrey*, Edgar I. and Jane R. Stewart, editors, Champoeg Press, Portland, Oregon, 1957 (Kicking Bear, A. R. Waud)

Graham, Col. W. A., *Abstract of the Official Record of Proceedings of The Reno Court of Inquiry*, Stackpole, Harrisburg, 1954

_____, *The Colors of the Seventh at the Little Big Horn*, Hollywood, California, 1952 (Elk Eber, A. Roloff, C. Lindeberg)

_____, *The Custer Myth*, Stackpole, Harrisburg, 1953 (Gayle Hoskins)

_____, *Official Record of a Court of Inquiry convened . . . upon the request of Major Marcus A. Reno . . .* Pacific Palisades, California, 1951

_____, *The Story of the Little Big Horn*, Century Co., New York, 1926; Military Service Publishing Co., Harrisburg, 1941, 1945

Grant, Bruce, *American Indians, Yesterday and Today*, E. P. Dutton & Co., New York, 1958 (B. J. Bjorklund)

Greenspan, Bud, "The Lone Survivor," *Coronet*, September 1956

Haines, William Wister, *The Winter War*, Little, Brown & Co., Boston, 1961 (R. M. Powers)

Hanson, Joseph Mills, *The Conquest of the Missouri*, Murray Hill, New York, 1946

Hawley, Maj. Gen. Paul R., "Did Cholera Defeat Custer?" *Surgery, Gynecology and Obstetrics*, May, 1947

Haycox, Ernest, *Bugles in the Afternoon, Saturday Evening Post*, Aug. 21-Oct. 9, 1943 (Donald Teague); Bantam, New York, 1961 (unknown); Montreal, 1962 (Frank McCarthy; New York, 1962 (McCarthy)

Heiderstadt, Dorothy, *Indian Friends and Foes*, David McKay, New York, 1958 (D. H. Miller)

Henry, Will, *Custer's Last Stand*, Chilton, Philadelphia, 1966 (Karl Wurzer)

_____, *No Survivors*, a novel, Random House, New York 1950 (Sofran); Bantam, New York, 1965, (N. Abbott)

Herndon, Booten, "From Custer to Korea," *Saga*, September 1961 (Ray Houlihan)

Herr, Maj. Gen. John K., and Wallace, Edward S., *The Story of the U.S. Cavalry*, Little, Brown, Boston, 1953 (White Bird, Leigh)

Hunt, Frazier, *Custer, the Last of the Cavaliers*, Cosmopolitan, New York, 1938 (John W. Thomason)

_____, and Hunt, Robert, *I Fought with Custer, The Story of Sergeant Windolph*, Scribner's, New York, 1947 (Thomason)

Hutchins, James S., "The Cavalry Campaign Outfit at the Little Big Horn," *Military Collector & Historian*, Winter, 1956

Indian Sign, May-June, 1951, Indian Drilling Mud Co., Oklahoma City

Ingraham, Prentiss, "Buffalo Bill's Gallant Stand," *Buffalo Bill Stories*, no. 95 (Edward Johnson)

_____, "Buffalo Bill's Grip," *Beadle's Weekly*, Jan. 13-Mar. 10, 1883 (unknown)

_____, "Buffalo Bill with General Custer," *Buffalo Bill Border Stories*, no. 200, 1914 (color cover)

Irvine, Ernest A., *The Benton Murals in the Missouri State Capitol*, Vandalia Leader, 1939

Jackson, Donald, *Custer's Gold*, Yale University Press, New Haven, 1966

Johnson, W. Fletcher, *Life of Sitting Bull*, Edgewood, n.p. 1891 (Little Big Man)

Josephy, Alvin M. Jr., editor, *The American Heritage Book of Indians*, New York, 1961

_____, and Lavender, David, *The American Heritage History of the Great West*, New York, 1965

Kelsey, D. M., *Our Pioneer Heroes and Their Daring Deeds*, Scammel & Co., St. Louis, 1882; reprinted as *History of* the *Wild West and Stories of Pioneer Life,* Thompson & Thomas, Chicago, 1903, variant illustrations

Kennedy, John F., *Public Papers of the Presidents,* 1963, Washington, 1964, pp. 502, 737-38

Korn, Jerry, "Custer's Last Stand," *Collier's,* June 30, 1951 (William Reusswig)

Krakel, Dean, "Mr. Leigh and His Studio," *Montana,* July, 1967

Kuhlman, Charles, *Did Custer Disobey Orders at the Battle of the Little Big Horn?* Stackpole, Harrisburg, 1957

_____,*Custer and the Gall Saga,* Billings, Montana, 1940

_____,*Legend into History,* Stackpole, Harrisburg, 1951

Leigh, W. R., "My America," *Arizona Highways,* February, 1948

Leighton, Margaret, *The Story of General Custer,* Grosset & Dunlap, New York, 1954 (N. Eggenhofer)

_____, *Comanche of the Seventh,* Farrar, Straus, New York, 1957 (Elliot Means)

Libby, O. G., editor, *The Arikara Narrative,* North Dakota Historical Collections, 6, Bismarck, 1920

Life Treasury of American Folklore, Time, Inc., New York, 1961 (James Lewicki)

Lizorty, Ken, *June 25, 1876, Custer's Last Stand,* Hazelwood, Missouri, 1966

Lossing, Benson J., *Our Country,* Johnson & Bailey, New York, 1895, III, (F. O. C. Darley)

Luce, Edward S., *Keogh, Comanche and Custer,* St. Louis, 1939 (Elk Eber, Rico Tomasco)

Mace, William H., *A School History of the United States,* Rand, McNally & Co., Chicago, 1913 (Colby)

Marquis, Thomas B., *Custer on the Little Bighorn,* Lodi, California, 1967, reprints of six pamphlets published 1933-34

_____, *A Warrior Who Fought Custer,* Midwest Co., Minneapolis, 1931 (Wooden Leg)

Mattes, Merrill J., "Follow the Sioux Indian Warpath," *Holiday,* June, 1946 (Lyle Justis)

McCracken, Harold, *The Charles M. Russell Book,* Doubleday, Garden City, New York, 1957

_____,*Portrait of the Old West,* McGraw-Hill, New York, 1952

_____,*Frederic Remington, Artist of the Old West,* J. B. Lippincott, Philadelphia, 1947

McCreight, M. I., *Firewater and Forked Tongues,* Trail's End, Pasadena, 1947 (Russell)

McVey, Everett E., *The Crow Scout Who Killed Custer,* Billings, Montana, 1952 (Stanley Legowik)

Meadowcroft, Enid Lamonte, *The Story of Crazy Horse,* Grosset & Dunlap, New York, 1954 (William Reusswig)

Merington, Marguerite, *The Custer Story,* Devin-Adair, New York, 1950

Miers, Earl Schenck, *Our Fifty States,* Grosset & Dunlap, New York, 1961 (Eleanor Mill)

_____,*The Rainbow Book of American History,* World, Cleveland, 1955 (James Daugherty)

Miller, David Humphreys, *Custer's Fall,* Duell, Sloan & Pearce, New York, 1957 (Miller); Bantam, New York, 1963 (unknown)

_____,"Custer's Last Stand—Legend or Blunder?" *Adventure,* June, 1959; same title, by Robert Crichton with David Miller, *Argosy,* May, 1956 (both Walter Baumhofer)

Milwaukee Art Center, *An Exhibition in Tribute to Richard Lorenz,* 1966

Monaghan, Jay, *Custer,* Little Brown, Boston, 1959 (White Bird)

_____,editor, *The Book of the American West,* Messner, New York, 1963

Montana, the magazine of Western History, Special Custer Edition, Spring, 1966 (McBarron, Ralston, Eber, C. C. Smith, Russell)

Montana Historical Society, *George Armstrong Custer and His 7th Cavalry at the Battle of the Little Big Horn,* Montana Heritage Series No. 7, Helena, 1955 (Ellsbury, Pedretti)

Morris, Charles, and Leigh, Oliver H. C., *The Great Republic by the Master Historians,* III, R. S. Belcher, New York, 1902 (O. Reich)

Murray, Robert A., *The Custer Court Martial,* reprinted from *Annals of Wyoming,* October, 1964

Neihardt, John G., *Black Elk Speaks,* William Morrow & Co., New York, 1932 (Standing Bear)

_____,*The Song of the Indian Wars,* Macmillan, New York, 1925 (Allen True)

Nelson, Bruce, "Scalp Scoop," *Adventure,* April, 1942 (I. B. Hazelton)

Newman, Edwin, "This Was Custer's Last Stand," *Everybody's Weekly,* April 14, 1951

Newsletter, Little Big Horn Associates, beginning January, 1967

Newsom, Thomas McLean, *Thrilling Scenes Among the Indians,* Belford, Clarke & Co., Chicago, 1884

Nichols, Roy F., Bagley, William C., and Beard, Charles A., *America Today,* Macmillan, New York, 1938 (G. M. Richards)

Parker, Gilbert, *Tarboe,* Harper, New York, 1927 (Harry Cimino)

Parrish, Randall, *The Great Plains,* A. C. McClurg, Chicago, 1907

Parsons, John E., and duMont, John S., *Firearms in the Custer Battle,* Stackpole, Harrisburg, 1953 (T. B. Pitman)

Paull, E. T., *Custer's Last Charge, March-Galop Descriptive*, E. T. Paull Music Co., New York, 1922

Paxson, William Edgar, "Custer's Last Stand, The Painting and the Artist," *True West*, October, 1963 (E. S. Paxson)

Pearl, Jack, "General Custer's Last Day on Earth," *Saga*, February, 1958 (Borack, Underhill); *War Stories*, Spring, 1963 (Ray Houlihan)

———, "The Redman's Last Stand," *Saga*, November, 1960 (Thomas Beecham)

Place, Marion T., *Buckskins and Buffalo*, Holt, Rinehart & Winston, New York, 1964 (Paul Laune)

Potomac Corral of Westerners, *Great Western Indian Fights*, Doubleday, Garden City, New York, 1960 (Ray Houlihan); University of Nebraska Press, Lincoln, 1966 (E. S. Paxson)

Prebble, John, "Suicide on the Little Big Horn," *Lilliput*, April, 1955 (Raymond Sheppard)

Price, Will, "Lonesome Charley," *True West*, May–June, 1961 (Dave Kinney)

Ralston, J. K., *The Custer Mystery*, Custer Battlefield Museum and Historical Association, Inc., n.p., n.d.

Ramey, W. Sanford, *Kings of the Battlefield*, Aetna, Philadelphia, 1884 (H. M. Snyder)

Rawling, G. S., "Custer's Last Stand," *History Today*, January, 1962

Red-Horse, Sioux, "Battle of Little Bighorn," *Tenth Annual Report of the Bureau of Ethnology, 1888-'89, Washington*, 1893

Reeder, Armand W., "Custer's Last Stand and Anheuser Busch," *Traffic Club News*, St. Louis, March, 1954

Remington, Frederic, *Pony Tracks*, Harper's, New York, 1895

Reusswig, William, *A Picture Report of the Custer Fight*, Hastings House, New York, 1967

Reynolds, Quentin, *Custer's Last Stand*, Random House, New York, 1951 (F. T. Chapman)

Richeson, Voorheis, "Seventh Cavalry," *U.S. Army Recruiting News*, April 1, 1930 (White)

Robinson, Harry B., *Guide to the Custer Battlefield Museum*, reprint from *Montana*, July, 1952

Roe, Charles Francis, *Custer's Last Battle . . .* Robert Bruce, New York, 1927 (J. W. Evans)

Russell, Charles M., *Pen and Ink Drawings, Book No. 2*, Trail's End, Pasadena, 1947; reprinted (with Book No. 1) as *Forty Pen and Ink Drawings*, 1947

Russell, Don, "Custer, American Soldier, *Facts*, January, 1944 (Hall)

———, "Sixty Years in Bar Rooms; or Custer's Last Fight," *The Westerners Brand Book*, Chicago, November 1946 "More on Custer Art," July, 1948

Ryan, J. C., editor, *Custer Fell First: The Adventures of John C. Lockwood*, Naylor, San Antonio, 1966 (D.M. Yena)

Sabin, Edwin L., *On the Plains with Custer*, J. B. Lippincott, Philadelphia, 1913 (Charles H. Stephens)

Sanderson, Edgar; Lamberton, J. P., and McGovern, John, *Six Thousand Years of History*, E. R. DuMont, Philadelphia, 1899, III, (O. Reich)

———, *The World's History and Its Makers*, Universal, Chicago, 1900 Vol. III, (O. Reich)

Sandoz, Mari, *The Battle of the Little Bighorn*, J. B. Lippincott, Philadelphia, 1966 (Robert Hallock)

———, *Crazy Horse*, Alfred A. Knopf, New York, 1942

Scudder, Ralph E., *Custer Country*, Binfords & Mort, Portland, Oregon, 1963

Senarens, Louis Philip, *Custer's Little Deadshot*, Wide Awake Library, no. 826, 1888; reprinted as *The Boy Prairie Courier*, Pluck and Luck, no. 348

Seventh Cavalry, Seventy-fifth Anniversary, Fort Bliss, Texas, 1942 (Cassilly Adams)

Shea, Cornelius, "Young Wild West at the Little Big Horn," *Wild West Weekly*, no. 108, Nov. 11, 1904

Shiflet, Kenneth, E., *The Convenient Coward*, Stackpole, Harrisburg, 1961

Simmons, Gurden, and Meyer, Ralph Louis, *This Is Your America*, III, Literary Classics, Inc., New York, 1943, p. 101: " 'Custer's Last Stand' Is Still a Popular Painting," by Stanton G. Mockler, from the *St. Louis Globe-Democrat*

"Sitting Bull's Version of Little Bighorn," from *New York Herald*, 1877, *American History Illustrated*, August, 1966 (Hoskins)

Souvenir Album of Paintings by Chas. Schreyvogel, Chas. F. Kaegebehn, Hoboken, New Jersey, 1907

Souvenir, Pawnee Bill's Historic Wild West, n.d., 1893?

Souvenir Program, 75th Anniversary Battle of the Little Big Horn, Billings, Montana, 1951

Smith, Cornelius C., Jr., "Crook and Crazy Horse," *Montana*, Spring, 1966 (Smith)

Smith, J. Greg, "The Man Called Crazy Horse," *Outdoor Nebraskaland*, December, 1964

Smitter, Wessel, "The Red Warrior Who Licked Custer," *Coronet*, August, 1949 (ty.)

"Speaking of Pictures . . . ," *Life*, June 21, 1948

Special Exhibition Catalogue, St. Louis Museum of Fine Arts, Nov. 14, 1908 (J. H. Sharp)

Spofford, A. R., Weitenkampf, Frank, and Lamberton, J. P., *The Library of Historic Characters and Famous Events*, William Finley & Co., Philadelphia, 1895, X (Remington)

Stands In Timber, John, and Liberty, Margot, *Cheyenne Memories*, Yale University Press, New Haven, 1967

66

Stanley, Rev. E. J., *Life of Reverend L. B. Stateler*, Methodist Episcopal Church, Nashville, 1907 (E. S. Paxson)

Steckmesser, Kent Ladd, *The Western Hero in History and Legend*, University of Oklahoma Press, Norman, 1965

Steele, Joel Dorman, and Steele, Esther Baker, *Barnes's School History of the United States*, American Book Co., New York, 1919 (W. M. Cary)

Steffen, Randy, "The Custer Fight," *Horse Lover's Magazine*, May-June, 1967 (Steffen)

Stenzel, Franz R., "E. S. Paxson, Montana Artist," *Montana*, Autumn, 1963

Stephenson, Nathaniel W. and Martha T., *A School History of the United States*, Ginn & Co., Boston, 1921 (M. Britt)

Stewart, Edgar I., "Custer's Folly," *Real for Men*, May, 1956 (A. Leslie Ross, John A. Elder)

———, *Custer's Luck*, University of Oklahoma Press, Norman, 1955

Stirling, Matthew W., "Indians of Our Western Plains," *National Geographic*, July, 1944 (W. Langdon Kihn, One Bull)

Swaney, Alex Grant, "March to Glory!" *Western Horseman*, January, February, 1954 (George Phippen)

Taft, Robert, *The Pictorial Record of the Old West, IV Custer's Last Stand*, reprinted from *The Kansas Historical Quarterly*, November, 1946

Terrell, John Upton, and Walton, Col. George, *Faint the Trumpet Sounds*, David McKay, New York, 1966

Toole, K. Ross, and Kennedy, Michael, "E. S. Paxson, Neglected Artist of the West," "Frontier Vermeer," *Montana*, Spring, 1954

Travers, Col. J. M., *Custer's Last Shot*, Wide Awake Library, no. 1196, March 31, 1894

Triff, George, *Fighting Indian Chiefs: Crazy Horse; Sitting Bull*, Mt. Hawley Pub. Co., Peoria, Illinois, 1963 (Herb Tenney)

Utley, Robert M., *Custer and the Great Controversy*, Westernlore, Los Angeles, 1962 (J. R. Williams)

Van de Water, Frederick F., *Glory-hunter*, Bobbs-Merrill, Indianapolis, 1934 (Will Crawford)

Vestal, Stanley, "The Battle of the Little Big Horn," as told by Chief Joseph White Bull, *Blue Book*, September, 1933 (Charles Fox, Joseph White Bull)

———, "The Man Who Killed Custer," *American Heritage*, February, 1957 (Joseph White Bull, Red Horse, Remington)

———, *Sitting Bull, Champion of the Sioux*, Houghton Mifflin, Boston, 1932 (T. B. Pitman), University of Oklahoma Press, Norman, 1957

———, "Sitting Bull and Custer's Last Stand," *Adventure*, Feb. 1, 1932 (Harry Townsend)

Virginia Museum of Fine Arts, *A Retrospective Exhibition of the Work of John Adams Elder*, Richmond, 1947

Walker, Judson Elliott, *Campaigns of General Custer in the Northwest*, 1881; Argonaut Press, New York, 1966

Wellman, Paul I., *Indian Wars and Warriors, West*, Houghton Mifflin, Boston, 1959 (L. F. Bjorklund)

Wheeler, Col. Homer W., *The Frontier Trail*, Times-Mirror Press, Los Angeles, 1923; reissued as *Buffalo Days*, Bobbs-Merrill, Indianapolis, 1925 (T. B. Pitman)

Whitaker, Hilary, "The Slaying of Yellow Hair," *Kiwanis Magazine*, June, 1965 (Franz Altschuler)

Whittaker, Frederick, *A Complete History of Gen. George A. Custer*, Sheldon & Co., New York, 1876 (A. R. Waud)

———, *The Dashing Dragoon*, Beadle's Boys Library, no. 20, April 26, 1882; no. 36, Dec. 20, 1884

———, "General George A. Custer," *Galaxy*, September, 1876.

Wilcox, Ella Wheeler, *Custer and Other Poems*, W. B. Conkey Co., Chicago, 1896 (A. G. Schmidt)

Wilson, Gen. James Grant, "Two Modern Knights Errant," *Cosmopolitan*, July, 1891 (Remington)

Wilson, William R., "Saber and Tomahawk," *The West*, August, 1967 (Schreyvogel)

Wiltsey, Norman B., "Fighting Cheyennes," *True West*, Fall, 1953, (George Phippen)

Wright, Bob and Kathryn, *Montana—Territory of Treasures, People, Places, Events*, Gazette, Billings, 1964 (J. K. Ralston)

OTHER PUBLICATIONS OF THE AMON CARTER MUSEUM INCLUDE:

Paper Talk
Illustrated Letters of Charles M. Russell
Introduction and Commentary by Frederic G. Renner

The Artist's Environment: West Coast
Text by Frederick S. Wight

Appaloosa
The Spotted Horse in Art and History
Text by Francis Haines

Taos and Santa Fe
The Artist's Environment, 1882-1942

Frontier Guns
Commentary by John Graves

Walt Kuhn
An Imaginary History of the West
Foreword by Fred S. Bartlett

Santos
The Religious Folk Art of New Mexico
Essay by George Kubler

Peter Hurd
A Portrait Sketch from Life
Text by Paul Horgan

Standing Up Country
The Canyon Lands of Utah & Arizona
Text by C. Gregory Crampton

Todd Webb Photographs
Early Western Trails and Some Ghost Towns
Introduction by Beaumont Newhall

Quiet Triumph
Forty Years with the Indian Arts Fund, Santa Fe

Brett Weston Photographs
Introduction by Nancy Newhall

Georgia O'Keeffe
The Work of the Artist from 1915 to 1966
Commentaries by her contemporaries

Camposantos
A Photographic Essay by Dorothy Benrimo
Commentary by Rebecca Salsbury James and
Historical Notes by E. Boyd

T. H. O'Sullivan, Photographer
Text by Beaumont and Nancy Newhall
Published in collaboration with George Eastman House

Texas Homes of the 19th Century
Photographs by Todd Webb
Text by Drury Blakeley Alexander

Charles M. Russell
Paintings, Drawings, and Sculpture in
the Amon G. Carter Collection
A descriptive catalogue by Frederic G. Renner

Aunt Clara
The Paintings of Clara McDonald Williamson
Text by Donald and Margaret Vogel

Painting in Texas the Nineteenth Century
Text by Pauline A. Pinckney
Introduction by Jerry Bywaters

Dorothea Lange Looks At the American Country Woman
A Photographic Essay by Dorothea Lange
Commentary by Beaumont Newhall

BOOK DESIGN AND PRODUCTION: CRAWFORD DUNN ASSOCIATES, DALLAS
TYPOGRAPHIC COMPOSITION: JAGGARS-CHILES-STOVALL, INC., DALLAS
LITHOGRAPHY: ANCHOR PRINTING COMPANY, FORT WORTH
BOOKBINDING: UNIVERSAL BOOKBINDERY, INC., SAN ANTONIO

Russell, Don, 1899–
　　Custer's last; or, The Battle of the Little Big Horn in
picturesque perspective, being a pictorial representation of
the late and unfortunate incident in Montana as portrayed
by Custer's friends and foes, admirers, and iconoclasts of his
day and after. ₍Fort Worth, Tex., Amon Carter Museum
of Western Art, 1968₎

　　v, 67 p. illus. (part col.)　26 cm.

　　Bibliography: p. 61–66..

　　1. Custer, George Armstrong, 1839–1876.　2. Little Big Horn, Battle
of the, 1876—Pictorial works.　　I. Amon Carter Museum of Western Art, Fort Worth, Tex.　II. Title.